CHARLIE SOONG

CHARLIE SOONG

NORTH CAROLINA'S LINK TO THE
FALL OF THE LAST EMPEROR OF CHINA

E. A. Haag

ISBN-13: 9780692468777
ISBN-10: 0692468773
Library of Congress Control Number: 2015909645
Jaan Publishing, Greensboro, NC

Editorial assistance provided by Snowden Editorial Services

Cover Photo Courtesy of 5th Avenue United Methodist Church, Wilmington, North Carolina

To my parents, wife, and children

TABLE OF CONTENTS

PREFACE

―◦◦◦―

WHEN I MOVED TO TAIWAN to learn Chinese in 1996, I planned on staying only one year. One year, however, soon stretched into six. During that time I not only began dating the woman that is now my wife, but also grew to love Chinese culture even more than I did when I first moved to Taiwan. Among the many unique experiences I enjoyed while living in Taipei was living next door to the former official residence of the former president of Taiwan, Chiang Kai-shek, and his wife, Soong Mei-ling. Despite the fact that their home on the grounds was still inaccessible at the time, the beautiful park that surrounded it became a favorite destination of mine, just as it did for many of Taipei's residents. Almost by osmosis I learned about Madame and Chiang Kai-shek and how they came to be an important part of Taiwan's history.

Nearly a decade later my wife and I moved to North Carolina. Within months of moving, I unexpectedly crossed paths again with the family of Madame Chiang Kai-shek (Soong Mei-ling). This time, however, it was her father, Charlie Soong, whose name I came across while reading a local publication. Charlie had spent much time in North Carolina and Tennessee as a youth, and the more I read about him, the more intrigued I became.

The fact that Trinity College, the school that Charlie attended in North Carolina, was so close to my home was a coincidence I found difficult to ignore, and it eventually spurred me on to delve deeper into Charlie's story. As I did so, I discovered how much a thorough and up-to-date account of his life was lacking. One English language biography of the entire Soong family was written several decades ago, but much new information about Charlie Soong has come to light since that time. The time is right for a new biography of Charlie Soong that can not only set straight some of the myths and rumors that have persisted about him and his life, but also properly credit him for the critical role he played in the Chinese Revolution of 1911. Central to such a biography would be the important role of North Carolina in the development and education of Charlie Soong.

It is an unfortunate fact that while Charlie was one of the closest and most influential friends and supporters of Sun Yat-sen, the man who was the de facto leader of the 1911 Chinese Revolution (Xinhai Revolution) that brought down the last emperor of China and who is still looked upon as the father of modern China, he was quite literally erased from the files of twentieth century Chinese history because of his painful, bitter, and extremely personal dispute with Sun after the Chinese Revolution. Although it is Sun Yat-sen and Charlie's daughter, Madame Chiang Kai-shek, who have received most of the attention as legendary figures in modern Chinese history in recent decades, it is Charlie Soong who is as deserving as anyone of being called a national hero in China. The Chinese themselves are finally coming around to realizing Charlie Soong's significance after decades of silence. In just the past decade a major memorial dedicated to Charlie was built in his hometown in Hainan, China, and in 2011 the first major conference of scholars gathered with Charlie Soong as the main focus.

The first half of this book is set in the United States and chronicles Charlie's remarkable experience in North Carolina and, to a lesser extent, Tennessee. The latter half is set in China and chronicles Charlie's similarly remarkable life and experiences after moving back there in 1886. Charlie went to great lengths to maintain confidentiality and privacy once he began fully participating in Sun Yat-sen's revolutionary cause, however. While this air of extreme secrecy did indeed help to protect him in the event of a crackdown on revolutionaries at the time, it also means that there is very little for historians to grab on to in regards to Charlie's life at this time. The dearth of information creates a distinct challenge for any biographer of Charlie, but it does not render the feat impossible. Enough evidence still exists in letters, books, and other documents to catch a telling glimpse of Charlie and his life in Shanghai at the time.

Most of the research for this book was conducted in North Carolina. Duke University in Durham and the New Hanover Public Library in Wilmington were particularly valuable sources of archival information regarding Charlie Soong and his life in North Carolina. During the research process, I occasionally uncovered documents and newspaper articles that have never been published (or republished, as the case may be) pertaining to Charlie Soong. The discovery of these documents and articles was an exciting part of the research process, and helped to shed new light on an old subject. Recent Chinese language newspaper articles highlighting the increasing attention being paid to Charlie Soong in China were also instrumental in the writing of this book.

The hundredth anniversary of Charlie Soong's death is only a few years away. With all the recent attention he has finally been receiving in China in recent years, there is little doubt that he will finally be recognized for his critical role in the development of modern China after nearly a century of virtual invisibility. No less important should the memory of Charlie be to the residents of North Carolina who because of him enjoy a proud and unique relationship with China that the residents of few other American states are able to lay claim to.

INTRODUCTION

⟨⟨⟨⟨⟩⟩⟩⟩

IN 1943 MADAME CHIANG KAI-SHEK, the wife of the de facto leader of China, delivered a powerful speech to the United States Congress. In the speech she attempted to garner support for China in that nation's bitter struggle against Japan. Americans were delighted and amazed by the unusual spectacle before them. As if the Madame's delicate physical features and striking presence were not enough, she professed to be a Christian and spoke fluent English with the subtle, lilting intonation of a Southerner. How could it be that that this woman from China could speak so eloquently, dress so elegantly, and claim Christianity as her religion? They would soon learn that the truth was even stranger than fiction. Over the course of the next several years, Americans learned more about Madame Chiang Kai-shek and her story, but they remained largely ignorant of her father and his. It was unfortunate, for the tale of Charlie Soong remains one of the most remarkable in the history of Chinese–American relations.

When a Chinese teenager suddenly appeared in the port city of Wilmington, North Carolina, in the summer of 1880, he was the first Chinese person many of the locals had ever seen. Although he spoke only broken English, his warm and genial nature won him many fast friends. As the people he met attempt-ed to divine just where he came from and why he was in North Carolina, they developed as much of an attachment to Charlie as Charlie did to them. Julian Carr, the wealthy Durham tobacco magnate and industrialist, was surely among the most important individuals to establish a relationship with Charlie, and his in-fluence would have a profound impact on the Chinese youth, as well as China itself.

Charlie Soong was a missionary, a businessman, a father, a pro-education advocate, and a revolutionary. He is also often re-ferred to as North Carolina's first international student. Above all, however, he was a pioneer, and an almost forgotten one at that. While serendipity certainly played an important part in his life, especially while living in North Carolina, hard work and a keen intellect also did much to shape his life after his move back to China.

Charlie Soong first met Sun Yat-sen in Shanghai in the 1890s, and would quickly become an indispensible figure in Sun's revolutionary cause. He would act as Sun's treasurer in the movement and be saddled with the majority of the revolution's fundraising responsibilities (funds that often included Charlie's own money). His home in Shanghai would also become Sun's secret base for over a decade after Sun became a wanted man in China for his revolutionary activities. Only Charlie's bitter fall-ing out with Sun in the years after the 1911 Revolution prevented him from going down in history as a hero of the revolution. If Charlie's contributions to early twentieth century China and Sun Yat-sen's revolution were not enough to gain him a permanent place in the annals of Chinese history, several of his children, particularly his daughters, would go on to be some of the most powerful and influential women in Chinese history after being sent abroad to be the first Chinese women educated in America. "One loved power, one loved money, and one loved China," was the mantra that Chinese schoolchildren for generations learned about the Soong sisters. Despite its simplicity, it is testimony to the powerful influence they exercised in China in the twentieth century.

Much in the way of myth and legend has developed over the course of the last century about Charlie Soong, especially in his beloved North Carolina. This book endeavors to separate fact from fiction in regards to his remarkable life. It is also hoped that it will help in the effort to acknowledge the contributions of Charlie Soong in regards to his important role in the Chinese Revolution of 1911, and in the effort to recognize him as a unique symbol of the special relationship between North Carolina and China that has existed for more than a century.

CHAPTER 1

BOSTON CALLING

⁃⧟⃛⃛⧟⁃

I N THE SUMMER OF 1880 a Chinese teenager arrived in the port city of Wilmington, North Carolina, speaking broken English and carrying only a knapsack. Virtually no one in Wilmington knew who he was or why he was there. He was, in fact, the first Chinese person many of them had ever seen. His polite and amicable nature soon endeared him to many of the locals, however, and soon the young "Celestial" was serendipitously thrust into the center of one of the most remarkable stories in the history of North Carolina. It was not in North Carolina, however, that the young teen's American adventure began.

Boston Harbor was as bustling as any of America's ports in the late 1870s, with ships of every conceivable shape and size competing for space along the crowded wharf. In addition to the loyal legions of traditional multi-mast wooden sailboats, steamships were just beginning to come into their own at the time after gaining popularity in the American Civil War the decade before. Passengers and the shipping industry alike hailed the invention of steamships as a technological marvel not only because they allowed people to be less dependent on the moods and whims of Mother Nature, but also because they dramatically increased the speed with which one could make transoceanic voyages. The age of the wooden sailing ship was about to come to an end in the 1870s, and the era of steel steamships was already well under way.

When the captain and crew of the *USS Albert Gallatin* steamed out of Boston Harbor on a stormy day in March 1879[1], they were aware that the high winds and rough seas created by New England's infamous March gales were dangerous. Rescuing ships in distress though, in addition to stopping smuggling and enforcing maritime law, was part of their job as sailors in the service of the U.S. Revenue Marine (the forerunner of the U.S. Coast Guard), and every man on board the *Gallatin* knew better than to complain. Even so, after rescuing four distressed ships over the next ten hours, the captain and crew of the *Gallatin* quietly began wondering if their day would ever end. When nightfall brought news that there was yet one more ship in distress somewhere off the coast of Massachusetts, its situation more desperate than any of the ships yet rescued, they dug in their heels one more time and prepared for the worst.

When the crew of the *Gallatin* finally came upon the *Ligure*, "a huge schooner heavily loaded with lumber," it was already morning; the wounded ship was turned over on its side after taking on water in the violent storm-tossed seas all night. Although the ship eventually righted itself in the turbulent waters, it had sustained so much damage that it was essentially inoperable. Moreover, one crewmember of the *Ligure* had already lost his life owing to the violence of the storm during the dark night, and exhaustion and hypothermia were threatening to take the lives of many more. Without hesitation the crewmembers of the *Gallatin* bravely boarded small rescue boats and made their way to the side of the *Ligure*, taking aboard that ship's crew and the body of the deceased crewmember. When the captain and crew of the *Gallatin* finally pulled back into the safety of Boston Harbor later that day, they did so with justly deserved doses of pride and satisfaction.

One of those crewmembers reveling in a job well done was the same teenager from China who would later make his way to Wilmington. He had been hired to work on the *Gallatin* a mere two months prior to the rescue of the *Ligure*. His courage, stamina, and coolness under pressure on that fateful March day helped to cement the close bonds that naturally form between members of a ship's crew, and between a crew and its captain. Indeed, both the captain and crew of the *Gallatin* quickly learned of the young man's loyalty and work ethic that day. There was still a lot, however, that they didn't know. They didn't know, for example, where he was born, how he ended up in Boston, or why he ever left China. Most importantly, they didn't know that the friendly and polite teenager who was the newest member of the *Gallatin's* crew would grow up to be one of the most influential figures in modern Chinese history.

Boston Harbor in the late nineteenth century was a microcosm of America; the crews on boats like the *Gallatin* hailed from around the United States and from around the world. It was not only a proverbial melting pot of ships, but also a grand stage where passersby on a daily basis could view firsthand the unfolding of the timeless theme of the clash between the old and the new, between innovation and tradition, and between the past and the future. Such themes would resonate throughout the lives of the men and women who were born into this era of rapid industrialization and social change, regardless of where they lived. Some places experienced this conflict between tradition and progress more intensely than others, however, and one of those places was China.

A battle for China's very soul and future played out on a daily basis in the Middle Kingdom in the latter half of the nineteenth century as a string of wars and uprisings tore the country apart at the seams. The perpetual conflicts had many consequences, not the least of which was young Chinese men bursting forth from China like sparks from a blazing fire—all in search of a better life for themselves and their families. Indeed, the Chinese teenager who somehow landed onboard the *Albert Gallatin* just a few months before its heroic rescue mission in March 1879 was one of those sparks. His name was Charlie Soong. Or was it?[2]

For decades after his death, the truth behind the origin of Charlie Soong's name was obscured by equal doses of confusion and poetic license handed down from generation to generation. The fact that so many variations of his name existed confused things even more. Although most of the questions regarding the "real" name of Charlie Soong have been settled, it is not surprising that they went unanswered for so long. Charlie, after all, was raised speaking a southern dialect of Chinese, the native language in his birthplace in Hainan Province. When he arrived in America the English he learned was saturated in a thick Hainan accent. Furthermore, any attempted spellings of his Chinese name in English were not based on the transliteration systems in common use today (i.e., Pinyin), but were simply his best guesses at spelling Chinese sounds using English letters. Later in life, he would also learn the Shanghai dialect of southeastern China, which was probably accented with heavy doses of both his original Hainan dialect and English. Add on to all of these linguistic complications the traditional Chinese custom of taking on a new nickname at least once or twice in life, and it's a wonder that anything at all was ever found out about Charlie and the origins of his name.

Charlie Soong was born in the city of Wenchang (文昌), on the Chinese island of Hainan (海南) on October 17, 1861[3]. In the past the subtropical island of Hainan (literally translated "South Sea"), located off the southwest coast of China a few hundred miles from Vietnam, was hardly the vacation destination it has become in recent decades. The island's population consisted largely of Han Chinese merchants, fishermen, and farmers interspersed with local ethnic minority groups, aborigines like the Li, some of whom were regularly involved in violent clashes with Chinese troops, whom they considered invaders. Far from the reaches of China's capital, government officials in Beijing considered the island somewhat of a cultural backwater outside the boundaries of civilization. Like Taiwan, its distant Chinese island cousin, Hainan was largely considered a hardship posting by Chinese civil servants in pre-twentieth century China; it was, for lack of a better term, a "punishment posting" where misbehaving regional administrators were often sent. It was in this place that Charlie would spend the first fourteen years of his life.

Ironically, Charlie Soong was born neither with the name Charlie, nor with the name Soong. Rather, Charlie's given name at birth was Han Jiao Zhun (韓教準), second son of Han Hong Yi (韓鴻翼). At the age of fourteen he was sent abroad with his older brother to work as an apprentice for relatives in the East Indies (modern day Indonesia). Being Hakka, an ancient subgroup of Han Chinese known for their migratory tendencies, it was only natural that young Charlie eventually learned the ways of his relatives and ancestors. Although he stayed in the East Indies working for several years, he would routinely return home to Hainan every Chinese New Year to see his family. It was on one of these trips home that he made the acquaintance of the brother of his aunt (the Chinese are very specific about rankings and titles in family relationships, often to a degree that bewilders non-Chinese; in the name of such specificity, the man in question was the brother-in-law of one of Charlie's uncles). The distant relative was a recently established tea and silk merchant in the small but growing Chinatown section of Boston, Massachusetts. Business was good, he told everyone, but the fact that he had no wife or children was weighing heavily upon him. Having no son to carry on a family name was not only considered a great tragedy in China, but a curse in the eyes of most Chinese. Not only would the family name of Charlie's distant uncle be snuffed out upon the occasion of his death, but no one would be around to make offerings and sacrifices for him in the afterlife, essentially dooming him to oblivion for eternity.

Unfortunately, many men suffered this unfortunate fate in nineteenth century China as a result of a long held cultural preference for boys over girls that led to a population heavily skewed toward males. For a fortunate few, however, there existed one hope. That hope lay in another tradition involving friends or relatives who had several sons. It consisted of bestowing upon one of those sons the last name of a childless friend or relative. In addition to a name change, the new namesake would also sometimes informally adopt the son, especially if that person had the wealth or means to teach the child a trade or better look after him than his birth parents. Such was the case with Han Jiao Zhun (Charlie). After a lengthy discussion between Charlie's parents and the brother of Charlie's aunt, who was surnamed Soong (宋), it was decided that Han Jiao Zhun would now be known as Soong Jiao Zhun (宋教準), and that he would soon be moving to Boston to work with his very distant uncle.[4]

The fact that Charlie was handed over to a distant relative indicates that Charlie's parents were not wealthy. Indeed, his father is said to have performed various jobs ranging from making rope and brick to selling coconuts. In accordance with custom Charlie was likely entrusted to his distant relative in order that he might be taught a trade and have a chance at a semi-lucrative occupation, and the relative, according to the account of the family historian, was eternally grateful for the gracious and generous act. Had the "uncle" any hint of the streak of independence and ambition then nascent in his new apprentice, he may have felt differently. It is not known how Charlie himself felt about the arrangement, but it didn't matter, for the decision was irreversible.

In such a manner was Soong (formerly Han) Jiao Zhun's life laid out before him by his parents and his new guardian in 1878. Given that the young lad had no choice but to go along with the plan, his arrival in Boston in 1878 at the age of seventeen[5] was followed by a period of employment/apprenticeship at the tea and silk shop owned by his uncle/guardian in Boston's Chinatown. In addition to the tremendous culture shock, the first winter that Charlie experienced in Boston did not likely make for a quick and easy transition to America for a boy raised in the subtropical climate of Hainan. Spending most of his waking hours working in a tiny shop in the cramped and confining Chinatown section of Boston did little to add anything to his contentment with his new life abroad. Such experiences were perhaps enough to make Charlie begin thinking and planning for an eventual escape from the certain fate that awaited him in Boston. It was the unexpected appearance of two boys from Shanghai in Charlie's life, however, that would really begin to turn the wheels of Charlie's ambition and self-determination, and have a profound impact on the rest of his life.

B. C. Wen (温秉忠) and S. C. New (牛尚周) were teenagers that were part of an ambitious venture, the Chinese Educational Mission, organized by the Chinese[6] government in the 1870s to help modernize China's educational system and Chinese society in general. The CEM began in 1872 and eventually enrolled over one hundred Chinese boys and teenagers in American schools, primarily in Massachusetts and surrounding states. The program was highly successful; it allowed young Chinese to obtain a Western-style education that would have been impossible to acquire in China (the program was actually "too successful" in that it would later be discontinued as Chinese officials discovered the boys were becoming "too Westernized"). According to popular lore, it was the influence of New and Wen, who used to frequent the tea and silk shop where Charlie worked, that stirred Charlie's discontentment and longing for a better life, and motivated him to make his next move.[7]

Although Charlie was supposedly inspired by Wen and New to leave his "menial" merchant existence in pursuit of a higher calling and, more specifically, a higher education, no one really knows the details regarding Charlie's life at this time, nor the nature of his relationship with his guardian. Perhaps Charlie did plead with his uncle to receive an education, and perhaps he was turned down again and again. It is equally possible that he simply loathed his life in Boston, or that he did not get along with his adoptive uncle, or that he wanted to return to China. Regardless, Charlie found a way to leave.

Just how Charlie managed to find a job in Boston with the Revenue Marine is yet another mystery that seems lost to time. One popular account has it that Charlie stowed away onboard the *Gallatin*, but there is little evidence of this. It is more plausible that he merely observed the ship on a regular basis whenever it was docked in Boston Harbor and one day simply asked for a job. Boston harbor was, after all, one of the boat's regular stops on its route from Edgartown, Massachusetts, to Portsmouth, New Hampshire, and Charlie's magnetic yet polite persona (which would serve him so well throughout his life) often rendered him instantly likeable to those he met. In addition, half of Charlie's life had been spent on or near the ocean, and he certainly knew his way around a boat as well as any sailor. If he was thinking about a new line of work, it was only natural that he should seek it on a boat.

While it's true that the runaway version of the story is certainly more romantic, a Coast Guard report[8] issued in 1943 detailing Charlie's service in the U.S. Revenue Marine simply states that Charlie "went down to the government pier and boarded the *Gallatin*, while she was in port on a routine stop." There is no mention of Charlie being a stowaway at the time, and based on a photo of the *Gallatin* (the skeletal frame of which still lies at the bottom of the ocean off the coast of Gloucester, Massachusetts, after sinking there in 1892), it's difficult to imagine that there were many places to hide on the modestly sized vessel. At the time of his enlistment on January 8, 1879, Charlie was described as being approximately five feet tall, but no mention was made of his thick, black hair, his prominent lips, or his wide-set nose. Charlie gave his name as "Chai-jui" (pronounced "Chai-rui" in the Pinyin system), the Coast Guard report states—perhaps his best attempt to pronounce or spell "Charlie," a previously acquired English nickname. His last name was spelled as "Sun" in the ship's log (also likely Charlie or the captain's best attempt at rendering Charlie's surname "宋" into English letters).

Despite its trials Charlie Soong's life was punctuated by many fortunate twists of fate. The first of these twists unfolded when he set foot aboard the *Albert Gallatin* and was immediately given a job. The second twist occurred simultaneously, when Charlie met the captain of the *Albert Gallatin*, Eric Gabrielson. Captain Gabrielson was no ordinary American, nor was he a ship captain that sprang from typical American sailing stock. For starters he was an immigrant himself, hailing from Norway. He had already lived in America for two decades before he met Charlie and served in the Union Army during the U.S. Civil War in the 1860s. It was his experiences as an immigrant, however, that undoubtedly went a long way toward casting an empathetic eye to the plight of young Charlie.

Gabrielson was also a devout Methodist, another factor likely influencing his subsequent generosity toward Charlie. It is even possible that Gabrielson was no stranger to China and its plight, for Methodist missionaries began trickling into China as early as the first half of the nineteenth century. By the time young Charlie arrived in America in 1878, Protestant missions were rapidly expanding in China and the stories of American missionaries there were making their way into many churches in the eastern and southern regions of the United States. Converting the "heathen" Chinese to Christianity at the time was a central focus of many Protestant churches.

A ship and its captain were synonymous in the era of nineteenth century seafaring, so much so that a captain was automatically considered a good man if he ran a good ship. This heuristic view extended to the crew of a ship as well. "To recall the man is to recall the ship," wrote one Coast Guard official in reference to the *Gallatin* and its crew, and a "member of the crew of a good ship was regarded as a good man, no matter how lowly his position." This sacred trinity between a captain, his ship, and his crew was an eternal, unquestioned truth in Edgartown (where Gabrielson lived), and it applied to the captain and crew of the *Gallatin* as much as any ship. The fact that the *Gallatin* and Captain Gabrielson were held in the highest esteem in Edgartown meant that Charlie too was regarded with equally high esteem. Indeed, both the fearlessness and the work ethic that characterized Charlie Soong in later years were plainly evident during his time onboard the *Albert Gallatin*.

Regardless of the superficialities that may have brought together the captain from Norway and the teenager from China, a strong bond developed between Captain Gabrielson and Charlie Soong over the course of the next year that went even beyond the traditional bonds that typically develop between a boat's captain and crew. The *Gallatin* routinely stopped in Boston, but its actual homeport was Edgartown, Massachusetts, where Captain Gabrielson and his wife lived. After being hired onboard the *Gallatin*, Charlie eventually took to accompanying Captain Gabrielson to Edgartown on days off of work, which usually consisted of Sundays and holidays, and was introduced to the residents of Edgartown. Even more relevant to his future, Charlie also accompanied Captain Gabrielson to Sunday services at the local Methodist church in Edgartown. To say that Captain Gabrielson informally adopted Charlie after his enlistment on the *Gallatin* would not be stretching the truth; the bond between captain and crewmember became so strong that upon completion of his first year of service in January of 1880, Charlie reenlisted without hesitation. His reenlistment in the U.S. Revenue Marine, however, was not destined to end on a happy note.

———— ഇൽ ————

By the time the nineteenth century arrived, China had been a single unified nation—varying in size— for over two thousand years. The emperors that ruled China during these two thousand years came from one of nearly two dozen dynasties, all of which rose and fell over various spans of time, the last of which was known as the Qing (pronounced "ching"). Indeed, the pattern that often existed in China's long history in regards to the life cycle of dynasties continued with the Qing regime. After a violent and unstable beginning in its early years (mid-1600s), China under Qing control gradually stabilized and became stronger. Gradually, however, corruption and incompetence set in, and the central government in Beijing increasingly failed to meet the challenges that confronted it. By the 1830s China was again in trouble.

Many serious problems plagued China during the nineteenth century.[9] Overpopulation, foreign influence, a growing number of opium addicts, and reluctance on the part of Chinese rulers to adapt to the modern world all contributed to bubbling discontent among the Chinese population at large. Persistent oppression at the hands of foreign countries intent upon carving China upon into individual spheres of influence was particularly harmful to China's development at this time. Not only did Chinese have to sit idly by and watch their proud country be overrun by foreigners, but both their economy and society appeared to be falling to pieces before their very eyes. It was obvious to Chinese living in the nineteenth century that their leadership was failing them, and many responded the only way they knew how—with rebellion.[10] Nineteenth century China is so replete with rebellions that it is easy to lose count. Furthermore, the rebellions that did flourish were typically no ordinary garden-variety rebellions involving passive crowds or chanting protestors and punctuated by the sounds of occasional gunshots. Rebellions in nineteenth century China, rather, were rebellions in which casualties and deaths are listed not in terms of thousands, but millions. The largest of them all, the Taiping Rebellion (1850–1864), began as a pseudo-Christian protest led by a Chinese man named Hong Xiu Quan (Hong's bizarre claim that he was the brother of Jesus Christ only served to increase his fame and popularity and helped to make him an unforgettable figure in Chinese history). Although difficult to verify, estimates of the number of Chinese troops and civilians that died during the Taiping Rebellion run as high as twenty million, giving it the grim distinction of being one of the deadliest armed conflicts in world history.

It's little wonder then that many Chinese men left China in the nineteenth century. For some of them, the moves they would make overseas would be permanent, meaning they would never again return to China even if they wanted to. The majority of peripatetic Chinese that turned up on American shores in the nineteenth century, however, never planned on staying forever. Their plan was nothing elaborate: go to America, earn money for a few years, then move back home. Implementing the first half of this plan was usually not difficult. Carrying out the second half, however, was sometimes more challenging than it sounded.

The question remained open in the mind of Charlie Soong as his Boston days drew to a close. Would he be one of the fortunate few with an opportunity to return to China someday, or did his destiny lie in America, thousands of miles away from his family, his friends, and the land in which he was born?

CHAPTER 2

A WILMINGTON WELCOME

———∞∞∞———

CHARLIE SOONG MAY NOT HAVE felt lucky after arriving in Boston in the late 1870s, but he was. Even at the depths of his misery, he was infinitely more fortunate than many of his countrymen ever dreamed of being. Indeed, he was so far removed from the deplorable circumstances that many immigrant Chinese found themselves in other parts of the United States and South America at the time that he simply could not have imagined how bad things were for them.

A smattering of Chinese had set foot in the United States prior to 1850. In contrast to their successors, they were often treated with a sense of awe and fascination rather than hatred and discrimination. The first recorded female Chinese on American soil, for instance, Afong Moy, came to America in the 1830s, but she was neither a tourist nor an immigrant worker.[1] Rather, she was a museum display that was part of a cultural exchange hosted by a New York City museum. Essentially acting as a real-life mannequin, she sat quietly in her display booth dressed in traditional Chinese clothing while knitting or using an abacus so that American museum-goers could have the rare opportunity to see an actual "Celestial" woman in her "natural" environment.

There was also Chin Gan, a "double-jointed Chinese dwarf," who caused no less of a stir among New Yorkers fond of circus act antics. The excitement he aroused in the circus world was only matched by the fuss created in the academic world by the enrollment of one of the first Chinese students in America; Yung Wing (容閎) would eventually be the first Chinese student to graduate from a U.S. university (Yale in 1854), and be the individual responsible for the creation of the China Educational Mission that brought Charlie's friends, B. C. Wen and S. C. New, to Massachusetts.[2]

While Chinese people remained somewhat of a novelty in the eastern United States well into the second half of the nineteenth century, the excitement surrounding their arrival in other parts of the United States had long since faded, if it ever existed at all. Nowhere was this truer than in the western regions of America. Prior to the California Gold Rush, a pivot point in Chinese immigrant history in the U.S., the sight of a Chinese immigrant in America was as rare as the sight of an American in China. What started out as a trickle of Chinese immigrants into California during the Gold Rush, however, eventually transformed into a flood in the 1850s. Residents of southern China, desperate to escape the chaos increasingly gripping the nation, began hearing more and more of Jiu Jin Shan—Old Gold Mountain—otherwise known as San Francisco.

While rumors of free gold in America circulated around southern Chinese towns and cities and newly minted Chinese who had recently returned from California after striking it rich provided proof that there was some substance to the rumors, tickets on ships to California sold faster than they could be printed. In addition American labor recruiters at the time often set up shop in Chinese ports in order to recruit cheap Chinese laborers and send them back to America to work on projects such as the Transcontinental Railroad.

Some Chinese did meet with success early on in the gold rush game and became quite wealthy, but for most, their experience in America would be far more humbling. If they were able to make decent money in America, it was usually sent right back to family members in China, and the money was rarely acquired through the get-rich-quick scenarios that many Chinese so vividly imagined before ever setting foot in America. Instead of striking it rich overnight, most Chinese ended up having to toil in the farm fields, grocery stores, laundry establishments, or Chinese restaurants that proved to be the only vocational choices available to them.

The nascent tide of racism and bigotry against Chinese that commenced almost as soon as they began arriving in the United States in the mid-1800s initially focused on restricting Chinese access to gold mines through a series of hastily passed laws like the Foreign Miners Tax Law.[3] The law did not specifically mention the Chinese as the reason for its existence, but it didn't really need to when it stated that "popular sentiment dictated that gold should be reserved for Americans." The taxes it imposed on miners who were not U.S. citizens were so heavy that any Chinese still mining in the early 1850s had no choice but to drop their picks and gold pans and pursue other means of making a living. Some scattered in various directions, but many went to San Francisco and a handful of other West Coast cities and established the first Chinatowns, where they began engaging in the various trades they would be known for later in America.

Laws discriminating against immigrants in America became more blunt and aggressive as time passed, and they brazenly began attacking Chinese specifically. "Their presence here is a great moral and social evil," stated one law, and "a disgusting scab upon the fair face of society." A court decision that barred Chinese from testifying against whites in court served as a proverbial straw that broke the camel's back, resulting in a great exodus of Chinese out of California toward the Midwest and eastern states to cities like Chicago, Cleveland, and New York. The discrimination and racism that led them to leave mining, however, would not simply disappear as they fanned out across the country and into other professions. In fact, in years to come it would only get worse.

—∞∞∞—

Upon his reenlistment in the Revenue Marine in January 1880, Charlie perhaps had thoughts of a career in its service. His relationship with Captain Gabrielson was proving to be as solid as any he'd forged since arriving in America; it could have done much to help Charlie establish a seafaring career if that was what he wanted. Ultimately, however, none of it mattered, for almost as quickly as he entered Charlie's life, Captain Gabrielson disappeared. In May 1880, Gabrielson was suddenly transferred to another Revenue Marine ship, this time in Wilmington, North Carolina.[4] The news was perhaps as much of a shock to the Norseman as it was to Charlie, but such was the life of a captain in the Revenue Marine. Captain Gabrielson perhaps tried to make some arrangements for Charlie before shipping off to Wilmington, but he had no authority to transfer Charlie along with him. Accordingly, after saying their final good-byes, the captain and Charlie parted ways.

Charlie stayed behind in New England onboard the *Gallatin*, but he didn't stay long. In July 1880, he suddenly "requested a discharge from the Service" and he was duly granted one. According to the Coast Guard report, he "unquestionably made the request because Captain Gabrielson had been transferred to the cutter (ship) *Schuyler Colfax*, based in Wilmington, North Carolina." Again according to popular lore, Charlie stowed away yet one more time on another boat—this one bound for Wilmington, North Carolina; nevertheless, there is no verifiable historical evidence that Charlie stowed away. It is again just as likely, if not more likely, that he simply arranged for passage on a boat bound for Wilmington with some of the money that he had saved up through working on the *Gallatin*. Regardless, there is much evidence that "on the first of August, less than three weeks after his discharge from the *Gallatin*," Charlie "re-enlisted aboard Captain Gabrielson's new charge, the *Schuyler Colfax*, a 350 ton side-wheeler."

Whether or not Charlie Soong was the first Chinese person to ever set foot in North Carolina depends partly on how one defines "Chinese"—by birthplace or by blood. If it is the former, perhaps it is true. If it is the latter, then Charlie's arrival was not a first for the Tar Heel state. Charlie didn't arrive in North Carolina, in fact, until six years after the death of two Thai-Chinese immigrants to North Carolina who reign even more famous than Charlie Soong in the minds of many Americans. Chang and Eng Bunker[5] (aka the Siamese Twins), were born in what is now Thailand to ethnic Chinese parents. After retiring from the Barnum and Bailey Circus, where they worked as an immensely popular sideshow attraction, they moved to an area around Mt. Airy, North Carolina, just north of Winston-Salem. In a string of many coincidences with Charlie Soong, they too would be warmly welcomed by the locals in their respective North Carolina communities, exhibit an uncommon business

savvy, and prove extremely adept at adapting to American southern culture. (Remarkably, they would also father twenty-one
children between the two of them, the descendants of which still
populate the Mt. Airy vicinity.)

Located on the east coast of the United States roughly halfway between New York and Miami, the city of Wilmington, North
Carolina, was far from the largest of America's coastal cities in
the 1880s. It had, however, served an important role as a port
since before the American Revolution. Nestled near the border
between North Carolina and South Carolina, Wilmington is not
technically located on the coast. Rather, it is nestled on a narrow stretch of land between the coast and the Cape Fear River.
The downtown Wilmington area itself borders the river and is
dominated by low-level buildings as it gently slopes upward away
from the river. The large Victorian-era homes that dominate
the cityscape in Wilmington convey a sense of the importance
of history and tradition in the small coastal city. And although
all of the typical shops, industries, and amenities that could
be found in any port city could be found in Wilmington when
Charlie arrived, it was the churches of Wilmington, both in size
and number, that could not have escaped Charlie's eye when
he first arrived. Wilmington was indeed a city with a long and
proud religious history, and churches punctuated the landscape
of Wilmington as commonly as banks and gas stations would in
most cities in later years.

Life in the picturesque port city into which Charlie had
sailed in the summer of 1880 was typical for a city of its size.
Although Wilmington supported a major port and had a thriving downtown district, it was still small enough to be quaint and
welcoming and its residents took pride in their strong moral
fiber. Stories and articles that filled the town's newspapers in

the 1880s paint a picture of a small city where everybody knows everybody else, and the activities of local churches and their congregants were regularly reported. One editorial in the town newspaper at the time expressed concern for "Crazy Kitty," apparently the town pariah as a result of problems stemming from her apparent mental instability[6]; another editorial the following year questions "if there is another city with a population of eighteen thousand in the United States that is as orderly and well-behaved, as a general thing, as Wilmington,"[7] because it has been "nearly two weeks since there has been a police arrest or a case for trial before the Mayor." Yet one more article chronicles the account of what was perhaps the most serious crime of that month in which "two small colored boys" met "a colored girl" on the street and, after finding out she had twenty-five cents, "threw her down and took it away from her."[8]

If Captain Gabrielson was surprised by his transfer to Wilmington, he must have been even more surprised after returning from a hard day's work at sea to find Charlie standing at the end of a dock. Despite the fact that Captain Gabrielson was known as a "stern taskmaster and strict disciplinarian," he must have smiled at the sight of what was almost certainly the only Chinese person in Wilmington at the time. The feelings of loyalty, admiration, and respect that the captain had developed for Charlie during the prior year apparently all came rushing back at the sight of him, for it wasn't long until the good captain again hired Charlie as a "mess boy" upon his new steamship, the *Schuyler Colfax.*

For Charlie, a comfortable familiarity resumed after he began working again with Captain Gabrielson. As before, Captain Gabrielson worked with Charlie and became his de facto self-appointed guardian. And again, Gabrielson introduced Charlie to his friends and associates during days off from work. Still as staunch a Methodist as ever, it's not surprising that Gabrielson introduced Charlie to some of the many pious members of local Wilmington churches. Although Charlie may have been the first person from China that the church-going residents of Wilmington had ever seen, the existence of China was anything but a revelation to many of the church leaders in North Carolina at the time.

Methodism was just one of many branches of Christianity practiced in the American South at the time of Charlie's arrival in Wilmington. For countless decades, the great majority of Christians in the South peacefully prayed and worshipped within the confines of their own local communities without worrying much about what was happening on the other side of the world. Beginning in the nineteenth century, however, things began to change. By the end of the century such a passive attitude toward religion was a relic of the past. Far from being content reading scripture in the comfortable confines of their churches, nineteenth century Christians, especially Protestant Christians, became more and more ambitious in their evangelical endeavors, and their ambition was only seconded by their sense of righteousness and adventure. There had been Christian missionaries centuries before in history, but now it would be the Protestants that would be most passionately carrying the missionary torch. This was the era of "Onward Christian Soldiers," and few branches of Christianity lived out this hymn of zealous Christian devotion more than the Methodists.

Just like the Catholics centuries before, Protestant missionaries fanned out to the far corners of the world in search of converts to Christianity in the nineteenth century. Unlike the Catholics, however, it would not be only priests who would act as missionaries for Methodists, Baptists, and Presbyterians. For nineteenth century Protestants, missionary work was a labor of the common man. Anyone could do it—anyone, that is, who felt the calling and possessed a genuine thirst for adventure. Likewise, becoming a missionary in the nineteenth century was not only a duty, it was also an honor. And few places in the world at the time offered the opportunity to bestow honor upon oneself and one's religion more than China.

There are various accounts of how Charlie was introduced to the Fifth Street Methodist Church in Wilmington, some slightly more credible than others.[9] One such account has Captain Gabrielson introducing Charlie to an influential public figure in Wilmington by the name of Roger Moore, who then befriended Charlie and eventually served as the catalyst for what happened next.[10] Other accounts involve various individuals claiming to be the primary matchmaker responsible for "rescuing" Charlie and introducing him to the church. Regardless, there is less controversy about the importance of a Reverend Ricaud, who was to be the next crucial link in the support network that would be crucial to Charlie and his future.

North Carolina in the late 1800s no doubt had its share of ordinary, run-of-the-mill ministers. Reverend Thomas Page Ricaud was not one of them. His faith was instead forged in the fires of a life so wrought with mystery and adventure that it could rival the chronicles of a sixteenth century European explorer.[11] Born in Baltimore in 1817, he was orphaned at a young age and "adopted by relatives and taken to Mexico." Soon after adoption he was unexpectedly whisked off to Mexico City and educated there. He eventually began studying to be a Catholic priest at the University of Mexico, but somewhere along the line his studies were interrupted by one of the many civil wars in Mexico at the time. After apparently experiencing a change of heart in regards to the pacifist idealism of Christianity, he began fighting in the wars himself and was eventually wounded and captured. Both his innocence and his Catholicism claimed as victims in the revolution, he then moved to France, and then to Virginia. While in Virginia, he studied law and it was there that his supposed fiery conversion to Methodism took place. His newfound faith ran so deep and was tempered so thoroughly that the ministry was presumably the only calling appropriate for the newly branded convert.

"Uncle" Ricaud, as Charlie would later affectionately address the minister, was slender with dark hair that curled back on the sides of his head well into his later years. A full gray beard clung to his cheeks and chin while his warm, penetrating eyes and sagging eyelids betrayed both a sense of wisdom and exhaustion after a life of adventure and experience that few ever know. Undoubtedly sympathetic to the plight of the young immigrant who had washed up on the shores of North Carolina thousands of miles from home, Reverend Ricaud took a liking to Charlie soon after their introduction in the autumn of 1880. The fact that Charlie was from China, a country very much in the crosshairs of Christian missionaries at the time, only piqued Rev. Ricaud's interest all the more.

Whether it was the influence of Captain Gabrielson, a crewmate onboard the *Colfax*, or the Rev. Ricaud himself, somewhere along the line Charlie was profoundly influenced by the Christian values, rituals, and beliefs that surrounded him in Wilmington. So much so that his now famous conversion to Christianity was followed rather rapidly by his baptism into Christianity.

As one account has it, Charlie was baptized in Wilmington at a Fifth Avenue Methodist Church revival. One woman many years later recalled how "the Chinese boy shook hands with everyone in the house" in the celebration after his baptism, "telling each one how he had found the Savior, and how he wanted to go back to China and tell his people about the salvation of Jesus Christ." One Mrs. Howell also claimed to be present the night of Charlie's conversion and stated that "he seemed quite happy and his face was shining," and that at a Sunday afternoon meeting a few days later "he spoke of his gratitude to the members of the Church" and spoke of how he wanted to "secure an education so that he might return as a missionary to his native land."[12] (As proof that the legend of Charlie Soong is still alive and well in North Carolina, a 1995 letter to the *North Carolina Christian Advocate* claims that the Trinity United Methodist Church in Southport, North Carolina, was the sight of Charlie's actual conversion to Christianity during a revival held there by Rev. Ricaud himself on the night of October 31, 1880.[13])

Regardless of the time and place of Charlie's conversion to Christianity, his baptism occurred on November 7, 1880. An article in Wilmington's newspaper a few days before was terse but descriptive in its announcement of the upcoming ceremony. "A Chinese convert will be one of the subjects of the solemn right, being probably the first Celestial that has ever submitted to the ordinance of Christian baptism in North Carolina." On Tuesday, November 9, 1880, an announcement followed on page one of the *Morning Star*:

> The services at the Fifth Street M.E. Church on Sunday morning last, in connection with the baptism of the Chinese youth alluded to in our last, is said to have been exceedingly impressive. The young man, whose Chinese appellation was Soon assumed the Christian name in baptism of Charles Jones.

Considerable religious interest was manifested at the various services at this church during the day, and at night a mate of one of the vessels in port was, we learn happily converted.[14]

In addition to Charlie's baptism, another round of his seemingly never-ending name game was played that fateful night in November. In the baptismal announcement, the name "Soon" is used for the first time in print. It's not known whether it was Charlie or someone else who came up with this spelling, but it was a slight improvement over the old one in that it more accurately reflected the actual pronunciation of his Chinese name Soong. Charlie would continue using this spelling of his name for the next several years in all letters and correspondence. Historians have debated ever since, though, about just exactly where the name "Jones" came from. While some have suggested that it was just pulled out of thin air as a good, generic name that was chosen merely as a convenience, the rumor that Charlie chose the name in honor of one "Captain Jones" on the *Colfax* was one that just wouldn't die in Wilmington. Even decades after Charlie's death the rumor remained, and the debate continued about whether or not a Captain Jones ever existed at all.

Exactly who came up with the plan to provide Charlie with an education and to train him as a China-bound missionary has also been the subject of speculation. Rev. Ricaud was likely instrumental in the decision, but Charlie himself certainly would have played no small role. It is likely that once the idea was suggested by someone in Wilmington, it didn't take much to convince Charlie of its appeal. Missionary zeal seemed to come naturally to him, after all, and when the possibility of receiving an education was thrown in the mix along with the opportunity to return to China (to see his family), it must have seemed a dream to the young man; he had likely wondered if he was ever going to see his home and family again, and worried about how he would make a living if he did. Charlie's desire to return home, if only for a visit, and to work as a missionary almost certainly burned nearly as deeply as the convictions of his newfound faith.

CHAPTER 3

STUDENT MEETS MENTOR

———— ✺ ————

D URHAM, NORTH CAROLINA, IN THE 1860s did not have a
good reputation. The tiny hamlet was not large enough
at the time to be called a city, and many nearby residents
winced at the thought of calling the hodgepodge collection
of wooden buildings there a town.[1] After all, it was not strik-
ingly different in appearance or character from many of the
"Wild West" towns that were springing up in the western regions of America at the time. Durham, or Durham Station
as it was known before, was a gritty crossroads town that few
predicted would grow beyond the smattering of taverns, prostitution houses, and miscellaneous shops that gave it its identity. Residents of nearby communities like Chapel Hill, proud
home of the oldest public university in the United States, the
University of North Carolina, never looked forward to traveling to or through Durham.[2] The region's bumpy, rural dirt
roads guaranteed that the twenty-mile journey from Chapel
Hill to Durham was never an easy one, and most Chapel Hill
residents were aware that the journey from Durham to Chapel
Hill could be longer than the train ride from Washington,
D.C., to Durham. Indeed, few people cared much for Durham
in the 1860s, but that was about to change.

The proximity of Durham to Bennett Station, North Carolina, the location of the largest Confederate troop surrender in the American Civil War, was mere coincidence.[3] The influx of tens of thousands of Union and Confederate troops into the area in the spring of 1865, however, was not, and with the arrival of the troops came a sudden seemingly endless demand for commodities and products of every variety. It was the insatiable demand for one Durham commodity, in particular, that unintentionally sowed the seeds of its future success during this crucial moment in history, and helped to transform Durham from a tiny town to a major city. That commodity was Durham tobacco.

As troops on both sides of the war discovered, there was something special about Durham tobacco that made it better than ordinary tobacco. As the story goes, Durham tobacco had a distinctive flavor that troops on both sides of the Mason-Dixon Line had never experienced, and soon discovered could not be found anywhere else. Indeed, during the closing weeks of the war, troops were begging, borrowing, and downright stealing stashes of local tobacco by looting the warehouses of Durham tobacco factories. They liked it so much, in fact, that they were unable to forget about its unique flavor months and years after the Civil War ended, even after they fanned out across the country and returned home to places like Texas, Mississippi, Georgia, Pennsylvania, South Carolina, New York, and Ohio. They liked it so much that letters from around the country poured into the handful of factories in Durham, begging for more tobacco.

Tobacco companies in Durham naturally thrived in the face of such demand. Few thrived as well as the W. T. Blackwell & Co. Tobacco Factory, purveyor of the world famous "Genuine Bull Durham Tobacco," and few men worked harder or benefitted more from the seemingly insatiable demand than Julian

Shakespeare Carr.[4] Having grown up in nearby Chapel Hill, Carr was no stranger to Durham in the latter half of the nineteenth century. Handsome and sturdily built, his round face and deep-set eyes projected an image of confidence without any trace of braggadocio. The long, thick mustache that graced his faced most of his adult life added an air of amicability to his appearance. Often referred to as "General Carr" in his later years, Carr was not an actual military general at all. The monikor was bestowed upon him as a term of endearment and respect in honor of both his brief service in the Army of the Confederate States of America (as a private) and his lofty status in the Durham business community. Indeed, although Julian Carr was never a high-ranking military officer, it did not matter one bit in the eyes of the Durham community. His persistent popularity and tireless leadership made him an unquestioned leader in the Durham community. His generosity and popularity were not the only things that made him one of the most notable men in North Carolina at the time. By the 1880s Julian Shakespeare Carr had become one of the richest and most successful businessmen in the entire American South.

It is the logo of Julian Carr's W. T. Blackwell Tobacco Company, rather than the name, that is recognizable to most Americans even today. The giant red bull known as the "Durham Bull" pasted on roadside billboards and painted onto the sides of barns all over America is still fresh in the minds of many, and is as synonymous with Durham as Durham is with tobacco. It was the genius of Julian Carr that made the logo so ubiquitous, and made his company such a success. Carr's success did not surprise those that knew him though. The ambitious entrepreneur was intelligent, industrious, and hardworking, and his dedication to the Methodist religion kept him on the straight and narrow.

What was surprising was that one of his most enduring relationships would be with a young, penniless Chinese teenager who
quite literally drifted up onto the shores of his home state seemingly out of nowhere and initially, it seemed at least, with no particular destination in mind.

⸺⸎⸺

On April 20, 1881, approximately six months after Charlie
Soong's (Charlie went by the name 'Soon' at this time) baptism,
sandwiched between a short article about the "tremendous excitement at the foot of Princess Street" that was the result of a "chick-
en dispute" and another article about the Wilmington Produce
exchange, there appeared on the front page of the *Morning Star*
an article with the headline "Interesting Services—A Chinese
Convert To Be Educated For the Ministry."

> There were very interesting services at the Fifth Street
> Methodist Church Monday night, the occasion being a
> sort of farewell meeting. Preparatory to the departure
> from Wilmington of the Chinese youth "Soon," who was
> converted under the administrations of the Rev. T. Page
> Ricaud, about a year ago, and who, upon attaching him-
> self to the church, assumed the name of Charles Jones, in
> compliment to the boatswain of the revenue cutter *Colfax*,
> who has been a very dear friend of the young man, and
> who still feels a deep interest in his welfare.
> The young Chinese left for Trinity College yesterday
> morning, in company with Rev. Mr. Ricaud, where provi-
> sion has been made for his receiving a thorough theo-
> logical education, either wholly at that institution or in

part at Vanderbilt University, after which it is expected that he will return to China as a missionary and preach the gospel in that heathen land.

The meeting at the Fifth Street Methodist church was a very impressive one, and will not soon be forgotten by those who were present, touching addresses being delivered by the young Chinese convert and by his friend, the boatswain, who is also a zealous Christian man

This is the first instance in North Carolina where a Chinese has been converted to Christianity, and the case has therefore elicited a very profound interest in the religious community.[5]

The article, written only six months after Charlie's baptism, makes it clear that Charlie's friend and shipmate, Mr. Jones, was not only real, but was an important and influential figure in Charlie's life during his time in Wilmington. Only a month later, however, it would be the Durham business magnate Julian Carr who would become the most important figure in Charlie's life.

There is still some debate regarding exactly who was responsible for Charlie Soong's introduction to Julian Carr. One story has it that Roger Moore, the Wilmington local thought to be among the first to have befriended Charlie, was a colonel in the same Confederate cavalry division that Carr served in as a private. According to this story, Mr. Moore befriended Charlie and arranged for him to meet Julian Carr. Another story has it that it was Rev. Ricaud who contacted Braxton Craven, the famed president of Duke University's predecessor Trinity College, and inquired about Charlie's education there and about any possible benefactors who might be willing to foot the tuition bill. Most plausible of all stories, however, comes from the pen of James

Southgate, a towering figure in Durham's Methodist community, and subsequent lifelong friend of Charlie. A brief history of the Trinity United Methodist Church written by him in 1895 states that the week prior to Charlie's conversion at the Fifth Street Methodist Church in Wilmington in 1880, Charlie was present "at a meeting held by me at Southport (North Carolina)." At that time Charlie "came forward for prayer, but was not converted."[6] Having been thus introduced to Charlie, when the annual Methodist conference was held in Winston-Salem the following December and the topic of the Chinese convert in Wilmington inevitably came up, Julian Carr was likely immediately suggested by Southgate (both he and Carr were influential members of the Durham Trinity United Methodist Church) as a possible sponsor for Charlie.

Regardless of who it was, there is little debate about the fact that it was Rev. Ricaud who brought Charlie to Julian Carr's home on Durham's east side in April 1881, and that it was the first time Carr had met either of them.[7] There is also little debate that Carr, and just as importantly his wife, were duly impressed with both Ricaud and Charlie. In a letter written later by Carr, Rev. Ricaud was referred to as "the sainted man" who "came to my home to bring Charlie Soong, the Chinese lad that I adopted." He added, "We enjoyed his visit very much. My dear wife appreciated his finely educated mind..."

In the very same month that Ricaud and Charlie visited Carr, Durham also officially became the county seat of its own county, a political and administrative feat for which Carr was largely responsible. Young Charlie surely sensed the importance of the man into whose home he was suddenly thrust, but at the same time the warmth and sincerity that emanated from Carr and his wife set him at ease in a way that eventually made him feel at home. Soon Carr and his wife would take him into their home "not as a servant, but as a son."[8]

Charlie would remain with the Carr family for a stretch of several weeks while he waited for his official enrollment in Trinity College. Trinity College itself had been in existence for several years by the time of Charlie's enrollment under the diligent leadership of Braxton Craven, the man whose name is now synonymous with both Trinity College and, by extension, Duke University (in the years following Charlie's enrollment at Trinity, the college would relocate from Trinity to Durham, North Carolina, and eventually be renamed Duke University). During this relaxing time Charlie often played with the Carr children and became friends with the children of some of Julian Carr's closest friends and acquaintances in Durham, including Annie Southgate, the daughter of James Southgate.

Before he was twenty years old, the second son of Han Hong Yi had literally traveled as far from his humble hometown in China as he could possibly get, and had taken in every sight there was to see and every lesson there was to learn along the way. By this time, however, he was beginning to feel every mile of the tremendous distance between his humble Hainan hometown and Durham, North Carolina after so many years abroad. So much so that finding such warm acceptance by Rev. Ricaud, Julian Carr, and others in North Carolina at this critical stage in his life touched him deeply, and would be something he would never forget. So it was that in the spring of 1881 the next chapter of Charlie's Soong's new American life was about to unfold in Trinity, North Carolina, and nobody was more ready for it than Charlie Soong.

Trinity College was a well-known and well-respected institution of higher learning in the mid-to-late 1800s, but today all that remains of the college in the tiny crossroads town of Trinity is a school bell. The bell sits in front of what is now Braxton Craven Middle School as a subtle reminder of the small college with a big reputation that once stood on the site. In contrast to the typical development of most towns, the town of Trinity was named after the school that eventually became the town's main attraction just a few years before Charlie's enrollment there. According to the 1868–69 act of the North Carolina General Assembly that created the school and the town, the town was to "be two miles long from north to south, and one mile wide from east to west" with "the center of the Town to be the center of the principal College Building."[9]

Although a school had existed in the area for several decades, by the time Charlie Soong arrived in late spring of 1881, Trinity College was well established and its affiliation with the Methodist Church well known. The school was experiencing financial difficulty and low enrollment at the time of Charlie's enrollment, however, and its continued existence may not have been possible were it not for generous benefactors who helped to keep its doors open.[10] Ultimately, however, it was the tireless dedication of its schoolmaster, Braxton Craven, that allowed the school to survive and evolve into the model of higher education it eventually became.

Although the enrollment of a Chinese student was unprecedented in the history of Trinity College, the rigorous training of missionaries for the purpose of educating foreign "heathen" populations was not an entirely new concept in the tight-knit Methodist Church communities of America. Soon after missionaries began shooting off to the far-flung reaches of the planet in the earlier decades of the nineteenth century, they discovered that preaching the virtues and ideals of Christianity to local populations was of little value due to language barriers. Their efforts were even more frustrated by populations of people who lacked even the basics of any education. It rapidly became clear to such church mission administrators that the education and schooling of both missionaries and potential converts was mandatory if their efforts were going to bear any fruit at all. As a result, educating local foreign populations quickly became a priority for missionaries, and the education of missionaries in regards to foreign language training and foreign culture training became increasingly common as the nineteenth century progressed. Young Charlie Soong, without even the benefit of having been a proverbial sheep for even a full year of his young life, was now suddenly being groomed to be a shepherd.

It was Rev. Ricaud's idea to educate Charlie, and it was Julian Carr's generosity that helped pay for it. Now it was Braxton Craven's turn to shape and mold the impressionable young man into not only an educated leader, but into a galvanized Christian soul strong enough and worthy enough to spread the Christian Gospel to what was then popularly viewed as the largest and most concentrated "bastion of heathenism" on earth—China.

It's impossible to say whether Dr. Craven felt unduly burdened or intimidated by the task of teaching Charlie, who could barely speak conversational English at the time, much less read and write English at a level anywhere near that of other Trinity students his age. If he did at the beginning, such feelings eventually dissipated in the wake of Charlie's warm and easy-going manner. Dr. Craven worked diligently to bring Charlie up to the level of his classmates, but it was his wife who took on an even more influential role as Charlie's personal tutor. It was she who would end up tutoring him nearly every night in the quiet confines of her comfortable Trinity home, and it was she who would make all the difference between failure and success in regards to Charlie's immediate future.

As Charlie settled into student life at Trinity, his life finally resumed a familiar normalcy that he likely had not known since he left his home on Hainan Island as a young boy. His dream of an education was finally, if not miraculously, being realized. Such a time was the perfect opportunity to pen a letter to his parents back in China in which he could assure them for the first time in many years that he was not only alright, but thriving in America. Charlie addressed the letter not to his parents but to one Mister (Dr.) Allen, a leading American missionary in Shanghai whom Charlie hoped could forward the letter (and likely a translation of it) to his parents.

The letter was sweet and heartfelt, and one can quickly sense both the yearning Charlie felt to see his parents again and his enthusiasm for his newfound religion. The fact that Charlie wrote in English when his parents likely didn't speak a word of the language may seem odd, but it was not. Charlie received a limited education as a child. He may have learned to read and write basic Chinese, but whatever he learned was almost certainly forgotten (in the days before mass communication it was not uncommon for Chinese expats to forget how to speak Chinese after living abroad many years). The first section of the letter was a direct appeal to a Dr. Allen, someone who in years following would become much more familiar to Charlie, though not in a way he had hoped.

Mr. Allen
Dear Sir,
    I wish you to do me a favor, I been away from home about six years and I want my father to know where I am

and what I am doing, they living in South East China in Canton state called monshou County, they have junks go from Macow to Hanhigh about 6 days water, my father name is "Hann Hong Jos'k" in Chinese. I hope you will be able to it out where they are, I was converted few months ago in Wilmington, North Carolina and now the Durham Sunday School and Trinity are helping me, si I am in a great hurry to be educated so I can go back to China and tell them about our Saviour, please write to me when you get my letter, I ever so much thank you for it, good by.[11]

Yours Respectfully,
Charlie Jones Soon

The second section of the letter was addressed directly to his father in Hainan. The author of the book from which this letter was extracted was the son of a lifelong friend of Charlie who spent most of his life as a missionary in China.

Dear Father,

I will write this letter and let you know where I am. I left Brother in East India in 1878 and came to the United States and finely I had found Christ our Savior. God for Christ sake has meet in the way. now the Durham Sunday School and Trinity are helping me and I am in a great hurry to be educated so I can go back to China and tell you about the kindness of the friends in Durham and the grace of God. I remember when I was a little boy and you took me to a great temple and worshipped the wooden gods. oh, Father that is no help from wooden gods, if you do worship all your lifetime would not do a bit goods. in our old times they know nothing about Christ. but now I had found a Savior he is comforted me wherever I go to. please let your ears be open so you can hear what the spirit say and your eyes looks up so you may see the glory of God. I will put my trust in God and hope to see you again in this earth by the will of God. now we have vacation and I stay in Mr. J.S. Carr house at Durham. Soon as you get my letter please answer me and I will be very glad to hear from you. give my loves to my mother Brother and Sisters please and also to yourself. I will tell you more when I write again. Mr. and Mrs. Carr they are good Christian family and they had been kind to me before I know them. Will good by Father. Write to Trinity College, N.C.

Your Son.
Hann Cardson
Charlie Jones S

Charlie couldn't have known it at the time, but his letter would never make it to his parents. It wouldn't be until years later, in fact, that he would successfully reunite with them for the first time in nearly a decade.

⟠⟠⟠

Had fate delivered Charlie Soong to the doorstep of any other state besides North Carolina, he almost assuredly would not have had the chance to meet with the likes of Rev. Ricaud and Julian Carr. One of the many reasons for this was a seeming local indifference in North Carolina to the enormous tidal wave of prejudice and discrimination that was unleashed against Chinese in other American states at the time. Indeed, if Charlie had started his American journey in a state like California or Oregon, his fate would have certainly been more intertwined with the masses of struggling Chinese all over America at the time than with the local elite. Struggle, after all, was core and central to the identity of the Chinese in America ever since their arrival in the nineteenth century.

Chinese were a common sight in parts of California as early as the 1840s. Although it would take another couple of decades before the Chinese would make their way to other parts of North and South America, most Americans then had at least heard stories about the Chinese. As early as 1854, talk was in the air of bringing Chinese laborers, then referred to as *coolies*, to the American South to work on the plantations, as the realization was setting in there that slavery was a dying institution. Daniel Lee, editor of the Georgia-based *Southern Cultivator*, was an early proponent of the idea when he wrote in an editorial that the "growing policy of bringing agricultural laborers from Africa, China, and other Asiatic nations into the British West India Islands, Cuba, Central America and Peru deserves the serious consideration of readers."[12]

By the late 1860s Chinese laborers in small numbers were arriving in New Orleans to work in various fields and plantations in Louisiana and a few other Deep South states. When the U.S. government suddenly terminated the importation of such laborers over concerns that the importation of coolies had the potential to develop into a new type of slave trade, it seemed that the practice would be terminated forever. The tremendous demand for cheap labor to work the fields and plantations in the

South did not dissipate as time passed. Labor agents and entre-preneurs in the South were well aware of the reputation of the Chinese in the western U.S. states as cheap sources of labor; they had played a critical role in the construction of the momentous Transcontinental Railroad.

A convention held in Memphis, Tennessee, in July of 1869 for the express purpose of finding the "best and cheapest means of procuring Chinese laborers" proved to be more than just an empty exchange of words.[13] In 1870 hundreds (possibly thou-sands) of laborers were brought in from China to work in fields, on plantations, and on railroads in several Southern states. They were brought in to fill the void and do the work on farms, plan-tations, and railroads that had previously been done by slaves. Indeed, to all outside observers it looked as if entrepreneurs and planters in the South that were looking to do nothing more than replace African-American slaves with Chinese ones. They soon discovered the futility of such a plan, however.

Within one year of their arrival in the Deep South in 1870, most Chinese abandoned the jobs for which they were hired af-ter a series of conflicts and confrontations with employers over their maltreatment. Some Chinese left after realizing that their employers were either changing the terms of their contracts on them, and in doing so reducing their pay or extending their work hours. Others left because of the blatant disrespect and vicious maltreatment that was the consequence of even minor transgres-sions. In one instance, a group of Chinese quit after a member of their crew was shot dead by a white supervisor after a minor scuffle. While the majority headed north or west for hopefully greener pastures, a few enterprising Chinese remained behind.

The Chinese that remained in the rural South seemed to know instinctively that work in the fields was dead-end work with little potential for adequate remuneration, and they immediately set about pursuing more lucrative endeavors—a nearly impossible feat in an economy that was largely stagnant and in a society where social status was not something you earned, but something into which you were born. Ironically, the fact that most of the Chinese that remained in the South after the mass exodus could barely speak a word of English prevented them from being discouraged by locals from going through with such risky undertakings. The eventual result of their stubborn persistence was the establishment of what became somewhat of an institution in the Mississippi Delta region: the Chinese grocery. (Even today, the descendants of these intrepid Chinese can still be found in some counties in and around the Mississippi Delta, with most having maintained a clear and distinct Chinese identity in addition to their American one.)

Although the circumstances surrounding Chinese laborers in the South were often difficult, they weren't as bad as those in places like Peru and Cuba.[14] In Peru the vast majority of Chinese workers, often promised fair wages and working conditions when they signed contracts back in China, were shocked to discover the deplorable and inhumane conditions under which they found themselves; some of the worst consisted of spending long hours on coastal Peruvian islands scraping up bird guano, an extremely valuable commodity in the nineteenth century owing to its renown as a fertilizer of unparalleled quality. The large numbers of Chinese that emigrated to Cuba in the 1840s and 1850s fared little better than those in Peru, and that's if they were lucky enough to survive the journey there; as many as 20 percent of Chinese laborers headed to South America and the British West Indies at the time were thought to have died en route. While in Cuba, Chinese laborers did not have to worry about guano mining, but they did often work in conditions far removed from the promises made to them by foreign and Chinese labor agents back in China.

Despite the harsh conditions that most Chinese labored under in North and South America prior to Charlie's arrival, the situation was going to get a lot worse before it got better.

CHAPTER 4

A GREAT DEAL OF ATTENTION

⎯⎯ ∞∞∞ ⎯⎯

A S THE SUMMER OF 1881 rolled into autumn, Charlie gradually settled into a student lifestyle that allowed him to progress in his studies at a fairly rapid rate. His limited education at
the time of his enrollment, however, meant that he had an inor-
dinate amount of catching up to do. His departure from Hainan
Island as a boy likely coincided with the end of any formal education, a deficiency now compensated for by his boundless enthusiasm and endless optimism. At the time of Charlie's enrollment,
Trinity College consisted of just one three-story rectangular
building with a handful of classrooms, but its diminutive size
was in no way indicative of its ever-expanding stature and influence in North Carolina. More importantly for Charlie, Trinity
College was led by Braxton Craven, a man whose legendary status was already well established by the time Charlie arrived at
Trinity College in 1881. Indeed, no man is more closely associated with Trinity College and its success than Braxton Craven,
and few men likely influenced Charlie more during this critical
phase of his youth and development than the man who "never
had but one ambition…to make men."[1]

Sufficient credit has never really been extended to Braxton
Craven and his wife for shaping the character of young Charlie

Soong during his time at Trinity College. Craven was by all accounts a man who wasted little time seeking praise or sitting on his laurels. Rather, he was, according to one former student, "above all things, a builder of character, and supremely endowed with the power of discovering the secret springs of one's life, and of working upon them for good purposes."[2]

"He was a man of striking personal appearance," wrote Jerome Dowd, Craven's biographer, in 1896.[3] "Being somewhat short and heavy set, with a massive head, well rounded and covered with thick black hair." His forehead was "high and prominent," and provided shade to his "dark, deep set eyes." His nose was straight, but "short and broad." He also sported a "thin, classic lip," which was always "clean and shaven." Perhaps providing him with his most identifiable trait, a "short, chubby beard" covered the majority of his jaw and chin, while "the lines and muscles about his eyes and mouth expressed strength, and his countenance in repose was hard and severe." In colder months he often wore a black Prince Albert coat, a sartorial habit that Charlie Soong himself would eventually adopt after moving back to China.

On the surface Craven was the archetype of a traditional school headmaster lifted right from the pages of a Charles Dickens novel. If he had a sense of humor, it was one of his more closely guarded secrets. Craven, rather, was a serious man on a serious mission who had little tolerance for horseplay. "Sometimes hearing of some mischief making or disorder," recalled a former student, "he would boldly walk in upon the boys, and in his quiet and serious manner say: 'Come boys, come; this sort of thing simply won't do. None of you can afford to be wasting time in this way. Every man of you ought to be in your rooms at work. I trust I shall hear no more of this tonight.'"[4] What made such an approach to discipline effective seemed to be the calm and cool manner with which Craven dealt with all such situations, as "flying off the handle" appeared not to be a tendency to which he was prone.

In addition to the portrayal of Braxton Craven as a stern but cool educator, he also appeared to have something of a stereotypical absent minded professor air about him that led people, upon first impression, to gather that he was either egotistical or simply rude. "He often passed people on the streets and on the campus without speaking or lifting his eyes from the ground. It was very rare that he spoke to a student outside of his office. Even in passing professors in the halls of the college he would often not notice them." Craven's absent-mindedness and inattention in this regard were simply attributed to his tremendous powers of concentration, however. Although Dr. Craven's social skills may never have been perfect, his knowledge, competence, and abilities were never in question. Nor was his loyalty to either his students and his profession. "His control over his students was remarkable. They idolized him," recalled one student, while another insisted "no man ever 'got next to me like Craven.'" [5]

Dr. Craven undoubtedly made an impression upon Charlie, but it was his wife, Irene, who influenced him perhaps even more by tutoring him on a daily basis in what was assuredly a Herculean task that demanded calling upon reserves of patience that only a mother is capable of. Charlie's lack of English skills guaranteed that even the simplest of academic tasks outside the realm of mathematics was made infinitely more difficult. Charlie's brief education in China when he was a boy likely included large doses of mathematics and the Chinese language. Now his education consisted of even larger doses of English writing and grammar and Bible studies, in addition to at least some of the curriculum typical of the times including history, natural science, law, logic, Latin, Greek, rhetoric, the fine arts, theology, and a smattering of other subjects. Because of his lack of proficient English, however, such high level subjects were likely limited. If he was at all representative of a typical Chinese student at the time, rote memorization was likely a learning technique that he mastered early on, and surely contributed to his success at memorizing Bible verses regardless of whether or not he actually grasped their meaning.

One advantage to Trinity College for students easily tempted by distraction was its rural location. Route 62 quietly winds its way through the tiny hamlet that still today consists almost exclusively of farms and single-family homes.[6] Although Trinity's rural setting gave Charlie the chance to focus on his studies and improve his English, it didn't mean there wasn't time for fun. In the months after his arrival in Trinity, in fact, Charlie's new classmates initiated him into the local school with a Halloween prank that would involve a jack-o-lantern placed in his room one night. Upon returning to his room, Charlie discovered the jack-o-lantern quietly flickering in the corner while his classmates hid behind doors and furniture to watch. It was the first time Charlie had ever encountered a jack-o-lantern, and the sight of it caught him off-guard and rendered him temporarily speechless. As his mischievous classmates did their best not to laugh out loud, Charlie regained his wits, walked directly up to the jack-o-lantern, and punched it directly in the face. His classmates duly reacted with a communal outburst of laughter; the incident did much to bring Charlie into their good graces.[7]

Charlie was the first Chinese person to enroll at Trinity College, but he wasn't the first minority. That honor went to a group of Cherokee Indian students recently added to the school's roster, a result of a trend in America at the time. Educators believed that pulling Indian children out of their homes and "Westernizing" them was the most beneficial course of action for them. By all accounts Charlie was well liked and got along with other students at the school, due in no small part to his impeccable manners and ever-congenial manner. He dealt maturely and calmly with the occasional teasing that came his way, mostly in the form of the giggling and staring of local students still amused by the novelty of his physical features and the likely occasional reference to him as "Chinee," the popular if somewhat derogatory word at the time for Chinese immigrants. Regardless, any taunting and teasing of Charlie that did exist because of his ethnicity appears to have largely dissipated a few months after his arrival in Trinity.

On occasional weekends and during holidays, Charlie would travel back to Durham and stay in the house of his friend and benefactor Julian Carr. While there he would attend church on Sundays with the Carr family and while away the rest of the time playing with the Carr children, as well as the Southgate children. Lazy Sunday afternoons would include long, relaxing hours spent sitting, eating, and chatting about the events of the day around the Carr dinner table. Nanny Carr herself is said to have trusted Charlie so thoroughly that upon the waking of her baby every morning Charlie was with them, she would immediately hand it over to Charlie to rock in his arms and to sing his favorite lullabies to. During these weekend and holiday visits to Durham Charlie would develop a deep attachment to the Carrs that would endure for the rest of his life. In turn, Julian Carr would cultivate a genuine fondness for the young immigrant, and unwittingly influence him in ways both subtle and profound. Carr's family, friends, and business associates also became familiar sights to Charlie at a time when Durham was growing and transforming into the most exciting place in North Carolina, and Carr's business dealings were surely the topic of many a conversation in the Carr household.

Charlie was certainly a novelty and a curiosity to both his classmates and his teachers while studying at Trinity College. A classmate of his recalled many decades later that Charlie "attracted a great deal of attention from the faculty, the students, and the people of the village because of his racial contrast to the Caucasian and because of his exceptional sprightliness." He recalled Charlie quite clearly even several decades after attending Trinity with him.

> His stature was short, his complexion was brownish-yellow, and his eyes dark brown with less of the Mongolian slant than is usual among people of his race. He was very sociable, very talkative, and very playful. I remember teaching him the game of hop-scotch on the walk in front of the east door of the college building.
>
> While the boys were disposed to tease him and play all sorts of pranks upon him, he was very amiable, full of fun, and always ready to respond in a playful spirit.[8]

Owing to his lack of English language skills and academic experience, however, his classmates wondered on occasion just how Charlie gained admission to Trinity College, and whether or not he was capable of succeeding. Most of his classmates had been in school since they were young children, after all. Now young men, they were well educated in nearly every subject under the sun by the time they arrived at Trinity College. Charlie, on the other hand, had spent the last several years working in shops and on boats in various locales around the world. Charlie "did not make much headway with his studies," commented one classmate in later years, and "none of the students regarded him as endowed with superior ability or as animated by any ambition."[9] Even more poignantly, the classmate recalled him as "light-hearted" and "eager to spend his restless energy in talk and play," so much so that neither he nor his classmates ever "imagined that anything serious was going on in his mind or that he was destined to be a leader."

Charlie's first six months at Trinity College passed quickly. By the time spring of 1882 arrived he was already thinking about the end of the school year. "Commencement will be here in a short time," he wrote in a letter to a friend in Durham, and "we have to study heaps."[10] The letter's free and easy use of colloquial English offered proof that Charlie's language skills were improving. Soon after the letter was written, Charlie found himself passing the lazy days of a long awaited summer break, and he was scheduled for a visit back to the Carrs in Durham. While waiting, he said last good-byes to friends who were leaving Trinity for the summer and then spent time with students who lived in town. He also wrote at least one letter during this time. The letter was to his classmate, J. G. Hackett, who had recently returned home for the summer.

> Both of Misses Field are here yet. They will go home next Friday morning. I tell you they are very pleasant Young ladies I like them very much…Trinity is very pleasant now, but I don't know what it will be like after the girls go off… Miss Bidgood is here yet, I believed she will stay here until next month. She looks as pretty as ever. I went to see her and Miss Cassie some time since. She talk right lively. Golden,

I been had good times with the grils, all day long, never looked at the books hardly since Com (Commencement) except the Bible. everything is quiet now. Miss Mamie and two other grils gone to visiting last night we did had big time all the grils...We went to called on Ella Carr, and we had the best time you ever heard of it.[11]

Although Charlie's letter to "Golden" Hackett is replete with spelling and grammar errors, it nevertheless serves as testimony to the rapid progress Charlie was making in regards to his English language skills. The year before, he spoke only broken English and could barely write his name in English. After a year at Trinity, his writing skills were demonstrably improved. The letter also bears early witness to Charlie's fondness for socializing. Interestingly, one of the young ladies referenced in the letter, Ella Carr (Peacock), would astonish North Carolinians in the years just before the outbreak of World War II when she would reveal a secret about Charlie that had been buried in her dresser drawer for five decades.

Ella Carr's father, who was also Julian Carr's brother, was a professor at Trinity College at the time of Charlie's enrollment there. Ella was still living in the Trinity-High Point area of North Carolina in 1937 when an article appeared in the morning edition of the *Greensboro Daily* recounting her experiences with Charlie. Charlie often came over to the house to listen to her play the piano, she recalled, but her mother one day decided that she "had enough and told him to stop coming around the house so much." Charlie, it seems, was fonder of both Ella and her music than she ever knew because a few months after his departure from North Carolina she received in the mail a formal photograph Charlie had taken of himself (probably in

Nashville), looking dapper and impeccably dressed. Ella kept the photo for nearly five decades before showing it to anyone, including the local newspaper. In the newspaper article next to the photo, she briefly reminisced about her youth in Trinity and talked about her distant memories of Charlie Soong.[12]

Things seemed to be going along as planned for young Charlie as far as late July of 1882; his education at Trinity was bearing fruit beyond anyone's expectations. Indeed, the minutes from the Sixteenth Session of the Hillsboro District Conference of the Methodist Episcopal Church that met on July 20, 1882, indicated that Charlie's progress at Trinity was encouraging and expressed optimism in regards to his future as a China missionary.

> He has already attended one session at Trinity and the progress he has made in the English Language, and his devoted piety as a Christian, give promise of much future usefulness. His greatest desire seems to be to be able someday to return to China and tell his mother and father of Jesus and the resurrection; to convince them to throw down the tools of heathenism and the embrace the religion of the Bible. We as a Sunday School feel proud of our young charge and under the guidance of a Kind Providence we pray that Charlie may yet be a useful missionary.[13]

The summer of 1882 for Charlie passed as carelessly and as happily as that of any typical American teenager of the time. If Charlie could have had it his way, perhaps he would have chosen to pass every month of the year as he did during the early summer months of 1882. It was not to be, however.

The reports concerning Charlie's transfer from Trinity to Vanderbilt have spawned many rumors over the years. The fact that the Chinese Exclusion Act of 1882 was signed by President Chester Arthur into law the first week of May didn't seem to have any relevance to Charlie's situation, but it is impossible to be certain. The few accounts of Charlie's transfer that do exist simply and matter of factly state that Charlie was transferred because it was thought that such a transfer would more quickly bring about the achievement of his goal to become a missionary. One stated that he was transferred to Vanderbilt in order to gain more exposure to missionaries who were returning from China so that he might learn from their stories. The fact that Rev. McTyeire, the president of Vanderbilt University, was a close friend of Reverend Young John Allen, the head of the Methodist Mission in Shanghai, China, at the time, lends credence to this possibility. An alternate explanation has also come into play in recent decades that speculates that Charlie was transferred to Vanderbilt University as a result of being caught in some sort of romantic dalliance with Ella Carr. There is little to no evidence to support such speculation, however.[14]

The real factors underlying the decision to transfer Charlie are likely far more mundane. Vanderbilt University was discussed as far back as the spring of 1881 in the April 20 (Wilmington) edition of the *Morning Star* article as a possible destination for Charlie. The article declared that Charlie would be receiving a "thorough theological education" at Trinity College, "or in part at Vanderbilt University." It may have simply been decided by Charlie's teachers and benefactors sometime late in the summer of 1882 that the time was right for Charlie to move to Vanderbilt since the theological studies program there could better prepare him for life as a missionary. Trinity College, after all, had no theology program that could directly prepare Charlie for life as a minister or missionary; Vanderbilt did. A second important factor, however, was likely the health problems increasingly plaguing the president of Trinity College, Braxton Craven.

As early as June 1882, after attending the Methodist General Conference, Craven was beginning to "look worn" and "broken in health." His face "looked haggard, his eyes sunken, and the furrows of his face deep." He was on the verge of only his sixtieth birthday, but the many tumultuous and challenging years he faced as president of Trinity College were beginning to take their toll. Even a leisurely extended trip to a Stokes County, North Carolina resort area known as Piedmont Springs—its miraculous waters were claimed to be "positively curative of Anaemia, Chlorosis, Dyspepsia, Anorexia, Diseases of the Skin, General Debility, and Neuralgia"— failed to resurrect the health of the schoolmaster. Finally in September upon the advice of a friend, Dr. Craven took a trip to Baltimore with his son to consult a medical specialist who, though cheerful, confided in Craven's son that "the worst might happen at any moment."[15]

Contributing to the difficulties of Craven was an accident his daughter had suffered in 1881 while a student at Greensboro Female College. One night while sitting near the fireplace in her room, some sparks shot out and immediately engulfed her clothes in flames. By the time the flames were extinguished, "a portion of her body was burned to a blister." The burns were so bad that she had to move back home with the Cravens where she remained in their daily care well into the following year.

The Cravens spent much time and attention on Charlie while he was enrolled at Trinity College in order to try to help him succeed. By the summer of 1882, however, it was quite clear to both the Cravens and everyone that knew them that their burdens were becoming too great to bear. Dr. Craven's declining health was in and of itself a hardship and a strain enough to nearly break them. The time and attention that the Cravens could afford to spend on Charlie the prior year was now a thing of the past. If the Cravens couldn't look after Charlie at Trinity, then who would? This was likely the real question facing Charlie's benefactors as they decided his fate in the summer of 1882, just before his transfer to Vanderbilt University.

Regardless of who made the decision to transfer Charlie to Vanderbilt University, it was not a decision accepted easily by Charlie. He had, after all, developed a close relationship and deep attachment to the Cravens over the course of the past year, a year that was probably one of the most stable and satisfying of his entire young life. Now all of that was about to be pulled out from under him. According to a newspaper account of his departure published several decades later, "Charlie visited the Cravens and had to be convinced that the transfer was for his own good" and "he couldn't stop crying."[16] As a symbol of his gratitude, he gave Mrs. Craven one of the homemade hammocks that had become one of his trademarks (and a small source of income) in North Carolina (the hammock still resides in the Duke University Library today). Not soon afterward, Charlie Soong boarded a train bound for Nashville, Tennessee, a city nearly five hundred miles from Trinity, the town that had become his home.

Just a few months after Charlie's departure from Trinity, Braxton Craven returned home from a party with his wife and went to bed feeling tired and fatigued. After falling asleep, his daughter, who was watching over him, noticed that his breathing had become unusually heavy and called for her mother. As he got up to walk to the chair, "he fell forward upon his face" and "lay speechless and motionless on the floor." On November 7, 1882, Braxton Craven, the president of Trinity College and mentor to thousands of Trinity College students, including Charlie Soong, died.

———⟨≋⟩———

The world continued to turn outside North Carolina in 1881. It was the year of the legendary shootout at the O.K. Corral in the American West, and just a few months after Charlie's enrollment at Trinity College, President Garfield was shot by an assassin at a Washington, D. C., railroad station; he had been elected to the presidency only months before. He died of his wounds in September of that same year. Back in China, things had generally calmed down from the rebellions and violence that had plagued it in the 1850s and 1860s, the biggest of them being the cataclysmic Taiping Rebellion. For a brief time the nation even underwent a period of attempted revitalization, known as the "Self-Strengthening" movement, in which major players within Chinese leadership for the first time in history tacitly and reluctantly admitted that Western nations possessed knowledge and skills that were perhaps superior to its own, and began making efforts to learn from the West.

These "Self-Strengtheners" certainly did not include everyone in China's government, especially the deeply entrenched Confucian scholars who sincerely believed China superior to the West in every way, but there were enough influential scholars and bureaucrats to lend strong support to the movement.[17] The Self-Strengthening movement itself was at its core a reform program that focused on making China stronger through the study and adoption of Western technology and armaments, though other Western ways of thinking would naturally be a part of the process. It was during this movement that such progressive programs as the Chinese Education Mission (which brought Charlie's Boston friends B. C. Wen and S. C. New to New England as boys to study) were initiated.

In the fall of 1882, just as Charlie Soong began the difficult process of adjusting to life outside of North Carolina, another awkward Chinese teenager sharing much in common with Charlie was busy learning English and adapting to a foreign culture in the Pacific island kingdom of Hawaii. The boy was then known to his classmates simply as Sun Yat-sen (孫中山). Although only thirteen years old, he made the long-distance move from China to Hawaii in 1879 in order to be closer to his older brother.[18]

Born into a peasant family in 1866 in the village of Cuiheng, just a few dozen miles from the port city of Macao in southern China, Sun arrived in Hawaii on the coattails of his older brother, Sun Mei, who had already been there for several years and established himself as a successful merchant and businessman. After a brief visit back by Sun Mei to Cuiheng in 1878 to visit his family and marry a local girl, it was decided that both Yat-sen and his mother would move to Hawaii the next year in order to share in the success of his brother and enroll the younger Sun in a local school. It was surely not a decision made lightly, as two of Sun's other elder brothers had already died while living in California. Regardless, the younger Sun successfully made the move to Hawaii and began living with his older brother. Upon discovering that there were no Chinese schools in Oahu, the decision was made to enroll young Sun in a local Anglican missionary school, the Iolani School, as a board student. The school enrolled mostly Hawaiians and "half-caste" students at the time of Sun's enrollment, and classes were conducted in English with a curriculum that was distinctly Western-based.

For three years Sun remained at the Iolani School, where his immersion in both the English language and a Western core curriculum would shape not only his mind, but also his character. Firmly rooted in a childhood that was distinctly Chinese, Sun's identity would undergo a radical transformation with his exposure to Western concepts and values while still a teenager. As Charlie Soong was also discovering, such cross-cultural education was not unusual in the latter half of the nineteenth century owing to China's increased exposure to the West; China in the nineteenth century was, after all, being torn open at the time by foreign nations in a way that it had never known in its long history. While foreign powers rushed into the cracks and crevices of China created by the massive rupture, Chinese men spewed out at an almost equally powerful rate in search of work, education, and ideas. For better of for worse, such young men were unwittingly morphing into a unique hybrid of Eastern and Western cultures that would forever change the fate of China.

Finally, it was at the Iolani School that Sun was introduced to the religion that would profoundly impact his life. There among the swaying palms and cool ocean breezes "attendance at daily prayers and Sunday Service was compulsory." While there, he "became initiated into the Christian rituals" and was frequently given homework that included reading the Bible, a book which prior to his arrival in Hawaii was likely as foreign to him as the writings of Shakespeare or Twain.[19] While Christianity was certainly strange and novel to the young Chinese boy, it would eventually shape and influence him in ways that no one could have predicted.

CHAPTER 5

SO ALONE AMONG STRANGERS

∽∾∾∾

WHEN CHARLIE SOONG ARRIVED IN Nashville, Tennessee, to begin his studies at Vanderbilt University in the autumn of 1882, he was barely in his twenties. Surprisingly, however, he was already substantially older than the university in which he was about to enroll. Indeed, before Vanderbilt University became one of the finest institutions of higher learning in the American South, it was a small school with a small reputation. In the first year of its operation in 1875, it enrolled a mere 307 students. It had some advantages over its competitors, however, and one of them was its unique relationship with one of the wealthiest men in America, Commodore Cornelius Vanderbilt.[1]

The fact that Charlie Soong should eventually find himself at a university whose very existence owed itself to a string of coincidences and serendipities is appropriate. Charlie's entire life, after all, was built on a similar foundation. Although Charlie had no opportunity to meet Cornelius Vanderbilt himself, who died in 1877, it's safe to say he would have admired and respected him as he had Julian Carr.

Unlike Carr, Vanderbilt came into his wealth by way of the railroad and shipping industries, and his wealth was as vast as it was legendary. Philanthropy, however, never seemed to be something that concerned Vanderbilt until the years immediately preceding his death. It was just such a time that a Southern Methodist bishop by the name of Holland McTyeire happened to appear on the scene with the happy coincidence that his wife was a cousin of Vanderbilt's second wife. Upon the occasion of traveling to New York City to have a medical procedure performed, McTyeire's wife made arrangements for him to stay with the Vanderbilts. The story goes that McTyeire, who was at the time leading a movement to establish a university in the South with the support and backing of the Methodist Church, got along superbly with Vanderbilt, and soon after that visit Vanderbilt decided to donate the sum of one million dollars to McTyeire's newly established school. Both implicit and explicit in the donation was a supposed desire on Vanderbilt's part to help heal the wounds caused by the Civil War between North and South and to "contribute to strengthening the ties which should exist between all sections of our common country." Vanderbilt would not live to see the newly established school named after him, but his legacy would live on forever after.

Charlie's experience at Vanderbilt does not seem to have been characterized by the same sort of youthful exuberance that he exhibited so freely while living in North Carolina, despite the fact that he actually spent more time in Nashville than he did in the Tar Heel State. Partially owing to a fire in the early 1890s that destroyed many of the early files and documents at Vanderbilt, there exists little in the way of letters, stories, or anecdotes about Charlie and his days at Vanderbilt.[2] Despite the dearth of information about him at this time, however, the evidence that does exist suggests Charlie got along with his classmates and that both his language and preaching skills improved markedly.

"He was of a most genial and friendly nature,"[3] one classmate recalled in later years, while another, Mr. J. B. Wright, recalled that Charlie was "of a jovial disposition,[4] and very popular with all the students." Yet a third classmate, John Orr, recollected that Charlie "prepared his lessons well, passed all his examinations, and graduated with honor in his class of four in Theology."[5] In Orr's later years he also told of a particularly touching incident that involved Charlie and poignantly illustrated the loneliness and isolation he must have been experiencing on a daily basis at that time. "Some of the Wesley boys met on Sunday morning in the little chapel before breakfast for an experience meeting. One morning Soong got up and stood silent for a moment. Then his lips trembled and he said: 'I feel so little. I get so lonesome. So far from my people so alone among strangers. I feel just like I was a little chip, floating down the Mississippi River. But I know that Jesus is my Friend, my Comforter, my Saviour."[6] After this raw display of pure emotion, Orr recalled, Charlie's fellow students gathered round him and offered their support.

While at Vanderbilt, Charlie took courses in English, math, modern languages, systematic theology, moral philosophy, and church history. "He was not a highly successful student," stated one writer in contrast to the accolades of others, "perhaps because he was not better prepared when he entered the University."[7] A classmate of Charlie's, who later became the Theology Department Dean at Vanderbilt, echoed this sentiment. "His marks indicate that he was only an average student in the grades he received—which, however, is doing well for a foreigner, handicapped as he was by limitation in his command and use of English."

In between studying and preaching while at Vanderbilt, Charlie did manage to have some fun and fraternize with other students. One of the acquaintances he would make in his first few weeks while at Vanderbilt would in fact remain a life-long friend, something rendered easier by the fact that he became a missionary and moved to China soon after his Vanderbilt days. Indeed, William Burke not only lived in China for most of his life after moving there in the 1880s, but remained eternally fond of recalling his first meeting with Charlie that was the result of a dorm room practical joke. A description of it in Burke's biography depicts a delightful, if typically American, scene that could have taken place in the dorm room of any college anywhere in the country.

To carry out the elaborate prank, Burke set up in his room a small table with a blanket thrown over it, a flat iron, and a washtub full of water with a silver dollar sitting at the bottom. What potential prank victims could not see were the batteries underneath the table upon which the iron and washtub sat and the copper wires running from them to the flat iron. William invited his dorm friends into his room and told them to touch the "enchanted flatiron" that "came out of a witch's cave over in the Great Smokies." He further taunted them by adding that "anyone who touches it loses the power of his will" and offered to give the silver dollar to anyone brave enough to grab it while also grasping the flatiron. No one volunteered, so William invited the only Chinese person he knew in the room, or for that matter, in the entire school.

"How about it, Charlie?" Bill asked.

Soon stepped forward gingerly under the stimulus of being called. He peered cautiously at the iron and into the basin. There was nothing to arouse suspicion. So he gripped the iron's handle and plunged his other hand into the water. The jolt sent him back with a startled cry, leaving the dollar still resting on the bottom of the basin. His surprised look, though, faded into a warm, sheepish grin almost before Bill's laugh broke out. It was this never failing sense of humor that drew the two into close friendship from their first days together at Vanderbilt.[8]

The playful scene reinforces Charlie's reputation as a fun-loving, easy-going youth who was never too busy to engage in a prank when the moment was right—even if he was on the receiving end of it. This endearing quality itself seems to have done much to help him turn acquaintances into friends. Indeed, William Burke would not only become a lifelong friend of Charlie's, but his friendship and influence would be the primary reason why Charlie Soong would one day choose to send his daughters to college in Macon, Georgia—the hometown of William Burke.

The 1870s and the early 1880s was a period of relative, if temporary, stability in China. The disastrous rebellions and uprisings of the previous two decades were still fresh in the minds of most Chinese, but the relative peace and calm that ensued allowed the Chinese bureaucrats and leaders to concentrate on China's future for once rather than spending all of its time fighting political, military, and social uprisings. However, when the 18-year-old Tongzhi emperor of China was rumored to have died in 1875 because of his "wild living and overindulgence in the pleasure quarters of Peking," and the emperor's throne was immediately occupied by a three-year-old child by the name of Guangxu (光緒), concern temporarily mounted that chaos was about to return to China once again.[9] Fortunately matters stabilized fairly quickly when Guangxu's aunt Cixi (慈禧) became the de facto emperor (otherwise referred to as the empress dowager), a position she would hold for more than three decades. It was a job for which she was well prepared. She was essentially already the leader of China for more than a decade (while Tongzhi was still a child), a time during which she first displayed publicly that her intelligence and talent were only matched by her cunning. The Empress Cixi would reign with unexpected gravitas over all of China in the latter half of the nineteenth century, and would do more than anyone else to shape the culture and environment against which Sun Yat-sen and his fellow revolutionaries would rebel in the decades before and after the turn of the century. Cixi was indeed a talented and capable ruler, but she also had her weaknesses—the biggest one of all being a penchant for conservatism at a time when almost all the rest of China was begging not just for progress and transformation, but for revolution.

Cixi may have been strongly conservative in her political orientation, but she was also keenly aware that indifference to public opinion would not benefit her long term. For this reason she allowed some of her key ministers to carry out surprisingly progressive policies. Diplomatic relations with Western countries like America and France were formally established for the first time in history in the 1870s (prior to this it was not seen as necessary to establish such egalitarian relationships with foreign countries, which were considered by Chinese officials to be inferior to China). A program of industrial and entrepreneurial reforms was also established, as the Chinese recognized the value of Western industrialization and technology for the first time. As it turned out, however, the introduction of such progressive policies, instead of placating increasingly discontent Chinese entrepreneurs and intellectuals, only whetted their appetite for change even more; among the ranks of the increasingly discontent was none other than Sun Yat-sen, the future leader of the Chinese revolution.

In 1883 just as Charlie Soong settled into a routine at Vanderbilt University, the innate rebelliousness and nascent discontent of a young Sun Yat-sen—his trademark in years to come—was about to manifest itself for the first time. Its roots lay in a decision to remove Yat-sen from Hawaii and send him back to his hometown in China. Although his parents approved of the decision, it was likely heavily influenced by Sun's older brother, Sun Mei, who was upset by Yat-sen's interest in Christianity. The act of Christian conversion was, after all, in the eyes of good, solid, traditional Chinese folk for centuries a traitorous and extremely dishonorable act because of the fact that it necessitated abandoning the Chinese ancestor worship rituals that had existed in China for millennia. Accordingly, Sun Mei could think of no better way to express his disapproval of conversion and prevent Sun's further exposure to nefarious foreign influence than to ship him back to his parents in Cuiheng. If Sun Mei thought that his younger brother's rebelliousness would end with his move back to his humble hometown, however, he was in for a surprise.

Life in Cuiheng must have come as a shock to young Sun Yat-sen as he struggled to reconcile his recent experience as a student in an environment that idealized the cultural values of the West with the thousand-year-old rituals and customs that permeated the rural, peasant backwater town of his early childhood.

As Sun soon discovered, science, technology, and brazen individualism do not go hand in hand with ancestor worship and
all the other traditional modes of living that were the hallmark
of small town life in China. In the months after Sun's return
to Cuiheng, it was only a matter of time before "everything in
the village provoked Sun's indignation and mockery."[10] With the
help of a childhood friend, Lu Haodong, Sun went on a rampage
at a Cuiheng temple that apparently left no god or goddess un-
touched. Although locals likely were of the opinion that it was
young Sun that was broken, it was the statues of wooden gods
and goddesses at a temple in Cuiheng that bore the majority of
the damage that resulted from Sun's aggression. Together, the
two vandalized the statues of the deities at the temple to such
an extent that the locals "were certain that the foreigners had
poisoned Sun Yat-sen's mind."

It was not long before Yat-sen was apprehended by civil authorities for his temple desecrations, but he was not subjected
to any immediate civil punishment; it is likely, however, that his
parents were consequently obliged to remove him from the village, lest the village authorities change their minds or another
act of rebelliousness be committed by the young Yat-sen. Indeed,
instead of punishing him outright for the transgressions by sen-
tencing him to a season of hard labor in the fields, his parents
arranged for him to attend school in Hong Kong. In the spring
of 1884, he duly enrolled in Hong Kong's Government Central
School, a well-respected institution that would later become
Queens College.[11] The school would provide Sun with an environment in which he would again thrive by supplying him with
the elements of a Western-based curriculum. Sun's parents, however, were not quite through with their attempts to force Sun to
conform to Chinese customs. In 1885 he would wed a young lady

from his hometown, a marriage largely arranged by his parents. His new marriage and spouse would do little to curb his ways, however, and his parents presumably eventually abandoned hopes that their youngest would be 'normal' in any Chinese sense of the word.

CHAPTER 6

THE EASY CHAIR

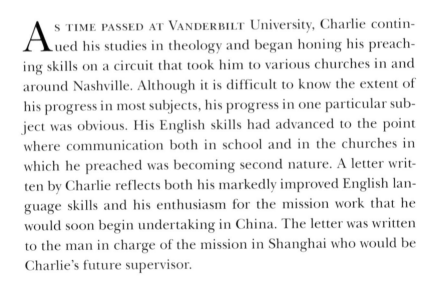

A S TIME PASSED AT VANDERBILT University, Charlie continued his studies in theology and began honing his preaching skills on a circuit that took him to various churches in and around Nashville. Although it is difficult to know the extent of his progress in most subjects, his progress in one particular subject was obvious. His English skills had advanced to the point where communication both in school and in the churches in which he preached was becoming second nature. A letter written by Charlie reflects both his markedly improved English language skills and his enthusiasm for the mission work that he would soon begin undertaking in China. The letter was written to the man in charge of the mission in Shanghai who would be Charlie's future supervisor.

> Wesley Hall, Vanderbilt University
> Nashville, Tennessee
> July 27, 1883

My dear Doctor Allen,

Your kind letter was received sometime since, and indeed I was very glad to get it. I see that you are fully consecrated your work, life, and spirit in God's hand. I hope to see you all soon by the will of God. I do not know how long I shall remain in the States, but I will try to prepare myself as thoroughly as the opportunity allow me. And when I ended my school days I hope that I will be able to carry the light to the Chinese. The object of my days is to do good, to honor man, to glorify God; to do good to others and save them from eternal punishment. God be my helper, I will. A few days ago, there was a Methodist lady asked me an uncommon strange question, said she "well, brother Soon, you are a missionary, will you suffer in any convictions and die for the cause of Christ?" And I thought it was a strange question to me. But, for the sake of my heart, I answered it according to my feeling. Replied I, yes, madam, I willing to suffer for Christ on any condition if God be my helper. Again said she "that is the way we ought to feel, for God will help us if we trust in him." May God help us all to lay our treasure in Heaven, and wait on him with great passion, and at least we may be able to say "I have kept the faith, I have fought the good fight, and henceforth I shall receive a crown of life." God bless you and all your labors.[1]

Charles J. Soon

It would be another two years after Charlie wrote the letter to Dr. Allen before plans for his actual deployment to China would begin taking effect. There is little in the way of stories or letters in existence today that can tell us much about these two formative years in Charlie's life, but its possible that this lack of information is evidence of Charlie's diligent application of himself to his studies during this time. One of the only surviving letters from Charlie while at Vanderbilt, written to his friend Annie Southgate in Durham dated April 24, 1884, bears testimony to the difficulty of the Vanderbilt curriculum and, once again, to Charlie's ever-improving language skills.

Dear Miss Annie,

It is true that I haven't written to you for some time; but you must remember I have written you a letter before I received this one. But you say, I ought to write whether receive the reply or not. Well yes, but I have 24 hours of recitations every week, and the lessons are exceedingly hard and long. In addition to the regular studies, 2000 pages of parallel reading to do during the session, and will have to stand an examination on this as well as textbooks. So you see I have a great deal to do during the year. I hope this will be a sufficient excuse to my most esteemed friend for my unpromptness. Our final examination will begin on the 8th of May and close on 22th (sic). I wish I have time enough to write you a long letter this very evening, but am not able.

You may look for a long letter from me about 24 or 25 of May. Yes, I am getting very anxious to see you all, but, my coming to Durham this summer is depend on somebody else, and not myself. I wish I have means to pay my way. I have to stand on all my examinations before long, so am not able to write you again until the examination is over. By the way, I have written a piece of play which I intended to send to you, but don't think, you will appreciate it because, no good thing is come out off "Nazareth", for the piece I have is my own originality. Gold (sic) to know you all were well. Please give my kindest regards to all.

I do not know exactly what I will do in the summer, but I had a plan fixed which I am expecting to carry out (if God wills it), and that plan is mental lecture. We have all kinds of gods in our reading room, and if I were to come to Durham next May, I will bring them with me, so you may have the pleasure of seeing them, or make a new acquaintance with the lifeless deities and learn of their character.[2]

Yours Truly,
Charles J. Soon

In addition to highlighting the difficult curriculum that Charlie faced at Vanderbilt, the letter also provides evidence that he was still making visits back to Durham during his years at Vanderbilt, and that his visits depended on Julian Carr footing the bill. The reference to "gods in our reading room" is presumably a reference to Chinese gods that missionaries headed to China would likely have been required to be familiar with as part of their training.

Despite his busy schedule in the days and weeks before commencement in the spring of 1885, Charlie took the time to write the first of what was to become a series of letters to the mouthpiece of the Methodist Church back in Raleigh, the *Raleigh Christian Advocate*. In the letter Charlie's enthusiasm for his newfound vocation is clear, and his English skills are better than ever.

My Dear Mr. Reid:

Nashville people are now doing good work in this city. The revival meeting began the latter part of last month and some of the churches had reached such result that never was known in the history of this city heretofore. The meeting is still going on in different churches, had 150 conversions already. In fact the success is greater than the expectation of the people. Rev. Mr. Sam. Jones, of Ga., (the Southern evangelist) will be in Nashville this week, and will preach in a "gospel tent," which will be erected in an open place by the post office.

This is a great blessing to the inhabitants of Nashville. We have not the least doubt, but that he will lead hundreds to Christ by the help and grace of God. If you want to know the result of the meeting, perhaps I can inform you, and it will be a pleasure for me to do so. I thank you for the ADVOCATE. Good by.[3]

Yours truly,
Charlie J. Soon

By 1885 Charlie had expressed a deep interest in studying medicine in order that he might be even more effective as a missionary in China. Even at this early stage it was likely that the ever-resourceful Charlie was doubtful of his ability to make a substantial living as a missionary in China and desired more practical skills to take back with him when he did finally make the move. He had even managed to garner the support of his mentor and sponsor, Julian Carr, who was willing to financially support Charlie in any medical studies he wanted to pursue. A superior at Vanderbilt, likely McTyeire, thwarted Charlie's personal ambitions, however, and prevented his enrollment in any sort of medical training program. The thoughts and attitudes expressed in a letter McTyeire wrote to Rev. Allen in Shanghai are, if not downright discriminatory, at the very least representative of an academic elitist view that Charlie, and by extension all Chinese, were incapable of making any worthwhile contributions to the missionary cause. The letter was written to Rev. Allen while Charlie's fate there was still being decided.

Vanderbilt University
Nashville, Tennessee
July 8, 1885

My Dear Dr. Allen:

We expect to send S*oon* to you this fall, with Dr. Park. I trust you will put him, at once, to *circuit work*, walking if not riding. Soon wished to stay a year or two longer to study medicine to be equipped for higher usefulness, etc. And his generous patron, Mr. Julian Carr, was not unwilling to continue helping.

But we thought better that the *Chinaman* that is in him should not all be worked out before he labors among the Chinese. Already he has "felt the easy chair"—and is not averse to the comforts of higher civilization. No fault of his.

Let our young man, on whom we have bestowed labor, begin to labor. Throw him into the ranks: no side place. His desire to study medicine was met by the information that we have already as many doctors as the Mission needed, and one more.

I have good hope that, with your judicious handling, our Soon may do well. It will greatly encourage similar work here if he does. The destinies of many are bound up in this case..."[4]

Yr. bro. in Christ.
H. N. McTyeire

Regardless of whether or not he was truly prejudiced, McTyeire clearly felt that "Chinamen" like Charlie needed to be "kept in their place," lest an inherent inner laziness be allowed to seep out under the temptations afforded by "the comforts of higher civilization"—as opposed to the presumably "lower" civilization from which Charlie sprang. In McTyeire's view Charlie was nothing more than a beast of burden whose purpose was simply to carry out the most physically demanding of tasks out on the front lines of the missionary world—often dangerous and exhausting work that McTyeire seemed to delight in forcing upon Charlie. It was a view that would naturally exclude him from any sort of leadership position (and its concomitant salary and status), and an opinion of him that was worlds removed from his North Carolina friends and mentors, most especially Julian Carr. The view was also bound not to go down well with Charlie, but would hang over him like a black cloud after his eventual move to China.

Even if it can be argued that the exact words of McTyeire's letter are not discriminatory, it is far more difficult to argue against the intellectual snobbery and distinctly harsh and bitter tone of the letter. Whatever else, it is fairly clear that McTyeire did not hold Charlie in high esteem, and that he thought little of his potential. Unfortunately for Charlie, his future supervisor in Shanghai would feel little different, as would Vanderbilt University officials like George B. Winton. In a 1931 interview with the *North Carolina Christian Advocate*, nearly fifty years after he met Charlie Soong, Winton recalled Charlie with a distinct tone of dismissive superiority.

> Soong, or Soon as we called him, was here from '82 to '85. He was a harum scarum little fellow, full of life and fun, but not a very good student. He gave no interest of having any serious interest in religion, even less in preaching. As a matter of fact, when he went back to China, Soon became interested in some business enterprise. In the course of time he married a woman who must definitely have been his superior.[5]

Regardless of naysayers, or perhaps because of them, Charlie "graduated" from Vanderbilt University in May of 1885 with an "English Theological Certificate." According to one source, however, the "degree received in 1885 represents three years work in the Theological Department" and "was a degree awarded to students who for reasons did not wish to continue the four years necessary for the degree of Bachelor of Arts."[6] If this is the case, it remains unknown why Charlie left Vanderbilt before obtaining the standard four-year degree, or if the choice was entirely up to him. Indeed, if Charlie was disappointed and upset over the decision not to allow him to pursue a medical degree, it would not be surprising if his anger motivated him to leave Vanderbilt before completing an official four-year degree program. At a farewell service conducted at Vanderbilt in 1885 for his benefit, no trace of bitterness was apparent, however, and his enthusiasm for his upcoming missionary venture was bubbling over. "I have been preaching some, and I have found pleasure and joy in preaching the Gospel of Christ. I go back to my people in China, to preach the Gospel of Christ to them, and to live the life of Christ among them."[7]

Before departing the United States, a return trip to North Carolina was in order for the purpose of his ordination as a deacon and for one more visit with the friends that meant so much to him. Not surprisingly, the residents of Wilmington, North Carolina, still took a noted interest in Charlie, and although he did not head there immediately after his graduation from Vanderbilt, the following article appeared in the Wilmington *Morning Star* on Saturday, June 20, 1885:

> Some years ago there was a Chinese boy employed on a revenue cutter on this station who visited the Fifth Street M.E. Church, became converted under the ministrations of the venerable pastor, Rev. T. Page Ricaud, and the members of the church all became very much interested in him, especially when it was discovered how intelligent and susceptible of mental improvement he appeared to be…

> ….On the 28th ult. (last month), as we noticed from a Greensboro paper, he graduated with high honors from the Vanderbilt University. He remains a few weeks with his friend and benefactor at Durham, and then, we understand, will go to China, where a professorship in the Anglo-Chinese University of Shanghai, Kingsi Province, has been tendered him. His conduct all through, we understand, has been such as to afford the highest gratification to those who have displayed a warm interest in his welfare, while towards those good friends he has always seemed to feel the deepest gratitude.[8]

It is obvious from this article that fond recollections of Charlie still lingered in Wilmington, but the fact that a mere two weeks after this article appeared in the *Morning Star*, Rev. McTyeire penned his harsh and bitter missive to Dr. Allen in Shanghai strongly urging that Charlie be "put…at once to circuit work," suggests much incongruity between words and actions among church administrators in regards to Charlie's future. Was McTyeire telling newspapers and congregants that Charlie was tendered a college professorship while simultaneously going to great lengths to make sure that he was assigned a job in the less esteemed and infinitely more labor intensive field of missionary circuit work? Or was the decision to put Charlie to work as a front line missionary made impulsively in the summer of 1885 after promises were already made to Charlie about a teaching position in China? Only McTyeire himself knew for certain.

Not surprisingly, Charlie's first stop on his return to North Carolina was Durham, where he undoubtedly stayed in the home of his benefactor Julian Carr. Charlie may have spent three years in Nashville, but his friendship with the Carrs and other Durham residents was as strong as ever. The generous residents of Durham were no doubt anxious to partake of the fruit of their labors, so it was that Charlie took ample opportunity to preach and prove to them that their efforts were not in vain. The following article appeared in the (Wilmington) *Morning Star* on July 9, 1885, under the title, "The Chinese Convert."

> Alluding to Charlie Soon, the Chinese convert, who went from Wilmington to Trinity College and thence to Vanderbilt University, the Durham Recorder says he preached in that place for the second time last Sunday to a "very large and appreciative congregation," and

continues: "He is a mere lad, but gives promise of usefulness as a minister of the Gospel, and will doubtless accomplish much good among his benighted race in heathendom. His discourse here yesterday was plain and practical, and he speaks distinctly, fluently, and with boldness."[9]

After Durham, Charlie moved on to visit Rev. Ricaud and the others who had been so kind to him upon his lonely and friendless arrival in Wilmington five years prior. Some have speculated that upon his arrival in Wilmington, an anxious and overprotective Rev. Ricaud had fears that Charlie had a crush on his daughter, and that, in response, he promptly whisked Charlie out of the city to a summer church camp. The facts, and a letter written by Charlie himself, prove otherwise. Ricaud wasn't even living in Wilmington at the time of Charlie's visit with him in 1885. In 1883 he was transferred to the First Methodist Church in Washington, North Carolina, and remained as minister there until 1886.[10] Charlie was indeed fond of Ricaud's daughter, by his own admission, but the idea that he was in amorous pursuit of her is dismissed by Charlie himself in a letter written by him in Plymouth, North Carolina, to Annie Southgate in Durham.

>...It took me three days to go from Durham to Washington, in which time I could have gone to New York City and back. I had a very pleasant time in Washington, although I know but a few girls as yet. They say there are seven girls to one boy, and some of them are very beautiful. I have fallen in love with Miss Bell. Don't you think that is too bad, for I have to leave my heart in Washington and I go to China.

There isn't any danger of my falling in love with any of Uncle Ricaud's daughters; Miss Jennie is engaging to a young fellow who is only seven feet and nine inches in height, and Miss Rosa is too young, for she is only 15 and has gone to her sister's to spend the summer. So you see there is no chance for me to fall in love, if I want to.

I suppose you are somewhere, wherever you may be, I hope you are having a nice time. Miss Annie, I must confess that I love you better and more than any girl at Durham. Don't you believe I do? I have exhibited my affection by writing to you through letter. I am spending a few days with Rev. Mr. Ware, who is a school-mate of mine at Vanderbilt. He is a nice young man.

I came here last Sunday. I shall leave Plymouth next Monday afternoon for Washington, and from there I will go to Greenville to visit another school mate of mine. And finally I shall proceed to Kenansville in Duplin to visit Mrs. Farrior, and I will deliver a lecture and preach there. Please give my kindest regard to all.

Please let me hear from you again. Direct your letter to Washington, in care of Uncle Ricaud.

Please interpret this word "Alllls" for me.[11]

Yours,
Charles

To be sure, Charlie's penchant for romance writing showed no signs of waning after his graduation from Vanderbilt, and his fondness for Rosamond Ricaud must have been genuine, for he would bestow upon one of his future daughters the (English) name of Rosamond (a few decades later, Charlie's daughters also reportedly visited Rosamond while attending school in America). He makes it clear, however, that he is also smitten with the recipient of his letter, his Durham friend, Annie, and one "Miss Bell" in Washington. In 1943, over fifty years after Charlie's visit, a reporter set out to find out who the mysterious Miss Bell was and whether or not she had any recollections of meeting Charlie. Indeed, she did. It was during the relaxed summer school session that the two met. "Practically every young girl and boy in the town attended," Mrs. Rowe (nee Bell) fondly recalled. Charlie's status as a foreigner only made him all the more special to the local children and teenagers, Rowe commented. And he "was regarded with the greatest respect, and admired for being ambitious and working his way through college." Furthermore, after commenting "he didn't look at all Chinese," she added that Charlie "dressed well" and had "beautiful manners." He was, indeed, "very, very polite, as the Chinese gentleman is noted for being." In testimony to Charlie's gentlemanly manner, Mrs. Rowe apparently never had any idea that Charlie liked her.[12]

According to his Vanderbilt classmate, Rev. D. H. Tuttle, who was assigned to the old Fifth Street Methodist Church in Wilmington where Charlie was baptized, Charlie did eventually stop in Wilmington on his farewell tour of North Carolina. "In 1885," Tuttle wrote, "during my first year at Fifth Avenue, he spent several weeks in my home, and the people of that church felt that he was their son in the Gospel...He preached for Fifth Avenue two or three times during his stay with me, speaking good English, and to the spiritual edification of all who heard him."[13] Charlie had indeed come a long way from his humble beginnings as a stowaway, and all of Wilmington knew it. But he was only just beginning.

Although Charlie Soong never lived in the American West, he surely could not help hearing or reading about the anti-Chinese violence taking place there at the time, especially in the fall of 1885. The Rock Springs Massacre in Wyoming and the anti-Chinese riots in the state of Washington, where the mayor of Tacoma reportedly declared that city's Chinese population "a curse" and "a filthy horde," led to the deaths of many immigrant Chinese in a climactic downward spiral of relations between local populations and immigrant Chinese communities that seemed to threaten the very existence of any Chinese population at all in America.[14] The majority of the violence, however, never made its way to the eastern United States, and this allowed Charlie to continue the lucky streak that was his trademark. Indeed, rather than being an outcast in the South, Charlie was now being called upon to fully participate in what was becoming a rush of sorts in the Methodist Church to send as many missionaries as possible to China as soon as possible. One of many public pleas for China missionaries appeared in the *Raleigh Christian Advocate* under the heading "150 Missionaries—The Call".

We propose this week merely to set forth the call which is made upon us as a church in behalf of the only pagan nation for whose redemption we of the Southern Methodist Church are laboring. Dr. Allen, Superintendent of our missions in China, most if not all his associates in that field concurring, call for 150 men and women to be sent to that mission during the next five years, beginning in 1886...For this purpose single men and women for the greater part are wanted—persons of robust health and robust conscience as well—persons of cheerful disposition and tough, tenacious purpose, with mental qualities and education acquirements not of the highest order, such as might be necessary in the hospital or college, but such as belong to men and women of good strong common sense, and understanding well the English language—China is no place to go to learn English.[15]

The article seems tailor-made for Charlie, almost suspiciously so. The terms "young, healthy, cheerful, and tenacious" could not describe him any better, after all, and the comments about needing people with "common sense" rather than those with academic skills and educational achievements "as might be necessary in the hospital or college," as well as "a good grasp of English" (an odd inclusion in a newspaper that was printed and published in America and intended for American readers), seemed explicitly written for Charlie. Regardless, it was into this hurricane of enthusiasm for frontline mission work in China that Charlie was about to be thrust, but not without first being officially ordained a minister in the Methodist Church. That ceremony would take place in Charlotte, North Carolina, when the 49th Session of the North Carolina Annual Conference of the Methodist Episcopal Church convened on Wednesday, November 25, 1885, at Tryon Street Methodist Church. On the third day of the conference, Friday, November 27, "Charles Jones Soon" of "Durham Station, Durham District" was admitted into the Methodist ministry.[16]

The following month, Charlie departed from Nashville bound for China. His train journey would take him across the Great Plains of the United States in a day and age when Indians and buffalo were still roaming in abundance. It would be a trip that Charlie would recall with great fondness in later years despite the anti-Chinese sentiment that prevailed in the West at the time. Eventually Charlie's train would wind its way to San

Francisco, and from there a steamer would slowly but surely carry him off to yet another new chapter in his life. Only in his twenties, Charlie had already seen more of the world than most people see in their lifetime. In addition he was now a full-fledged member of a small and unique breed of Chinese that could call two widely divergent cultures "home." He certainly anticipated his return with a great deal of excitement, not only for a reunion with the country of his birth, but also for the new vocation on which he was about to embark. Just as likely, however, his journey was rife with the trepidation and doubt that accompany all such major life changes. What he likely did not expect was the reverse culture shock he was about to experience in China. He would discover not only the incongruities that existed between his old memories and his new experiences there, but realize that the only thing that changed more than he did since his departure was the country he had left behind.

⎯⎯∞⎯⎯

In the mid 1880s the first cracks were beginning to appear in the makeshift foundation upon which China perched in the second half of the nineteenth century. As if the ailing nation had not had enough of the problems caused by the intrusion of Western countries into its internal affairs, another fateful incident occurred that would have repercussions for years to come.

Although the Chinese military conflict with the French known to historians as the Sino-French War actually began in 1884, skirmishes would continue until their conclusion a year later. The conflict may have been relatively brief, but it had been brewing for years as ever-expanding French interests in Vietnam finally reached a breaking point with Chinese government officials. Vietnam for centuries had been a sort of vassal state under the loose protection and control of China until the French began trickling in during the middle of the nineteenth century. There were a variety of reasons why the French were interested in Vietnam, but a key one was the access that control of Vietnam would allow merchants and traders to the populous southwest regions of China. Eventually, the verbal protests of the Chinese escalated into ground conflicts inside Vietnam itself, until the French took the war to a whole new level by attacking the Chinese navy at Fuzhou, an eastern port city on the other side of China from Vietnam. The attack took the Chinese navy completely by surprise and decimated it into near oblivion. A series of other French naval attacks, including one on the island of Taiwan, did much to assure a limited French victory, but it was a victory with casualties beyond the battlefield, and with ramifications that reverberated around Southeast Asia for nearly a next century.

The humiliation and shame that arose out of the ashes of the Sino-French War, especially the decimation of the Chinese army by the French at Fuzhou, were felt by Chinese all around the country. In Hong Kong the humiliation was even more acute. The recent widespread use of modern printing techniques meant that Hong Kong residents were more aware of current events in China. Such awareness gradually transformed anger into rage, and with the help of Chinese authorities in Canton who did everything in their power to inflame residents of Hong Kong against the French, riots soon broke out in the city that resulted in attacks on foreigners and a large-scale strike by Chinese shipbuilders and maritime workers.[17]

The strike itself, reasonably enough, centered primarily on a refusal by workers to repair ships arriving in the port of Hong Kong that needed repairs as a result of their recent conflict with

Chinese forces. If it wasn't for the strong reaction by British authorities in Hong Kong, the anti-French riots and accompanying strike may have lasted longer than they did. Regardless, the riots in Hong Kong were important and influential beyond the scope of the diminutive city. For one, they illustrated a growing sense of nationalism among the Chinese that had begun to slowly rise from the burning embers of the entire nineteenth century, which was such a disaster for China in terms of foreign relations. More importantly, the riots would provide young Sun Yat-sen with his first taste of Chinese nationalism and introduce him to the idea of using violence and mass uprisings to bring about change.

The years surrounding the anti-French riots in Hong Kong would be turbulent ones for Sun. After his arranged marriage in his hometown and his baptism in Hong Kong, his education at Queen's College would be interrupted by a demand made by his brother for his immediate return to Hawaii. Sun Mei did not call his little brother back because he was lonely. He called him back because he was angry. He was angry, in particular, that his younger brother had recently been baptized into Christianity. The baptism was salt in the wounds to Sun Mei, who had been angry about his younger brother's interest in Christianity for years. A year or two prior, Sun Mei gave half of his wealth and property to his younger brother in an attempt to help him "get his foot off the ground" in business and get him settled. No longer feeling so congenial, Sun Mei now not only wanted everything back, he duly told his brother upon his return to Hawaii that he was cut off from any further financial support. Sun was only able to return to Hong Kong with the help of a friend and minister, Rev. Francis Damon, who "raised $300 for Sun Yat-sen's journey back to China," and a childhood friend from

Iolani School who "gave his entire monthly salary of 5$" to Sun Yat-sen "for his trip."[18]

Sun's return to Hong Kong would be somewhat anticlimactic as his extended absence from the school where he was previously enrolled prevented him from simply returning to class as if nothing had happened. The young Sun was entering his twenties and seemed to have so little going for him in terms of career prospects that his family surely began to worry. According to one author, some of Sun's Christian benefactors had high hopes for his vocation as a preacher, and "Sun had probably encouraged him in this idea." Indeed, the money that Sun "requested from the Hawaii Christians were supposedly to allow him to return to Hong Kong to study theology." Afterwards, however, Sun never showed any further interest in pursuing a degree or a career in theology or the ministry.[19]

Instead of theology or the Christian ministry, Sun instead began looking toward medicine as a possible career. This led to his eventual enrollment in a medical school in Canton, where he was able to reunite with some of his childhood friends. His presence in Canton was temporary though as his application and acceptance to the newly established College of Medicine for the Chinese meant his immediate relocation back to Hong Kong.

The College of Medicine for the Chinese, which would later evolve into a branch of Hong Kong University, came about as project of the London Missionary Society. The main goal of the newly established hospital was to introduce and train Chinese students in the methods and practices of Western medicine, something that most missionaries felt was critically needed in China. It was certainly true that the Chinese had little in the way of Western medical techniques at the time, but most Chinese didn't want them. Western medicine, as was the case with so many other Western ideas and beliefs, was something that most Chinese looked down upon; the only kind of legitimate medicine in their eyes was the traditional Chinese medicine that had been in existence for centuries.

Western-style hospitals and science-based medical practices and procedures were just beginning to gather a modicum of respect in most Western countries themselves (anybody who could afford it paid for doctors to come to their homes; hospitals in nineteenth century America were shockingly filthy and occupied predominantly by the poor), so for them to make headway into China would take aggressive action. Sun was likely not pondering the ramifications of the lack of respect for Western medicine in China when he enrolled in the College of Medicine for the Chinese, but it was a fact that would have a profound influence upon not only Sun, but all of China.

Just as important as the curriculum that Sun would study at the College of Medicine for the Chinese would be the men with whom he would come into contact. The first of these men would be the director of the college, Dr. James Cantlie. Cantlie was a Scottish physician who had left his job as a surgeon in London to help establish and run the College of Medicine for the Chinese. He would take a shine to the young and ambitious Sun Yat-sen in much the same way that Julius Carr developed a pseudo-paternal relationship with Charlie Soong. He would become a friend and mentor of sorts to Sun during his college years, and his reappearance in Sun's life after a long absence would turn out to be the pivot upon which Sun's life would eventually turn.

The second person prominent in Sun's life at this time was a Hong Kong business leader active in the civic and political scene at the time, Ho Kai (the partial namesake of Hong Kong's gasp-inducing but now defunct Kai Tak Airport). Ho was another member of the small but unique subset of Chinese at the time who counted among their ranks the likes of Charlie Soong and Sun Yat-sen. All had studied abroad, all professed Christianity, and all returned to China with a passionate desire to shape it according to the their Western-based ideals. The ideas and beliefs of Ho Kai (何啟), in particular, would influence Sun Yat-sen, and the two men would go on to be friends and partners in their lifelong pursuit of an overthrow of the Qing Dynasty and the establishment of a Chinese republic.

CHAPTER 7

A FOREIGNER IN CHINA

⸺◦❀◦⸺

L OCATED ON A HARBOR APPROXIMATELY halfway down the
east coast of China, Shanghai welcomed Charlie Soong in
January of 1886 with a presumable lack of pomp and circumstance. After disembarking from the steamer ship that reunited
him with the country of his birth, he was overwhelmed by the
old, familiar sights and sounds of China. He may never have
been to Shanghai before, but just the sight of a busy street awash
with throbbing masses of Chinese and the ubiquitous signs covered in Chinese characters were enough to make his heart melt
and flood his mind with the rich memories of his childhood.

The smells and sounds of Shanghai itself lingered in the
air and surely struck a vein deep in Charlie's bank of memories
and brought at least one tear of joy to his eye. The unmistak-
able pungent odor of temple incense mixed with the smells of
cooking oil, garlic, human waste, opium, and the salty coastal air
of Shanghai was likely a frontal assault on his olfactory system.
Here an overzealous street vendor enthusiastically barking his
merchandise to throngs of passing Chinese; there two elderly
Chinese men talking over a cup of tea in a dilapidated, wooden
teahouse; and a little farther down the street a pack of stray dogs
fighting over a bone picked from street-side trash. Exactly what

went through Charlie Soong's mind as he walked the streets of Shanghai no one knows, but it was surely a memory in the making for Charlie. However much Shanghai reminded him of his childhood in China though, the fact remained that Shanghai in the late 1800s was not representative of China at large. There were parts of Shanghai, in fact, that were hardly recognizable as China at all.

Shanghai started out as a small Chinese settlement centuries before Charlie's arrival, complete with a city wall to keep out roving bands of Japanese pirates that routinely trolled the coasts in those days. Events in recent decades, however, had turned Shanghai upside down and inside out. The waterfront areas around the Bund in the late nineteenth century resembled old European cities more than any typical Chinese town owing to the influx of foreigners that began soon after the conclusion of the First Opium War in the 1840s. In fact, some parts of Shanghai were now devoid of Chinese themselves owing to the machinations of foreign nations that carved up Shanghai into various foreign concessions in treaty negotiations with China following the Opium wars. Large swaths of Shanghai, as a result, followed the laws and customs not of China, but of France, Britain, and the United States. It was into this cosmopolitan cluster that Charlie Soong was thrust his first day in Shanghai, and it was this same place he would one day call home.

It wasn't long after Charlie's arrival in Shanghai that he wrote the first of many letters from China back to the *Raleigh Christian Advocate* in North Carolina. The letter appeared under the simple caption, "A Letter from Charlie Soon."

DEAR BRO. REID: We have arrived in China now
a little over a month. All things being considered, our

trip has been quite pleasant to us. It took us twenty days to cross the Pacific, which was a little longer than we expected.

Upon our arrival at Yokohama, to our astonishment, we learned that the steamer, which we expected to make a direct connection for Shanghai, has left the harbor. In consequence of which accident, we were compelled to remain over in Japan for a week, and made the best use of our time. While there we went up to Tokio twice on the narrow-gate train and visited several places of interest, such as the National Education Museum, General Museum, Zoological Garden, and the Celebrated Buddhist Temple, which is known to the foreigners as "the morning grass."

The temple is quite ancient, but it is the most celebrated temple in the Capital of Japan. People go there from mornings to evenings to offer daily sacrifices and gifts. The day we were there, the "morning grass" was thickly crowded with the multitude. In their mode of worship there is one thing which deserves mentioning, and that is this: that no worshipper dared to bow to his god, nor would he be allowed to do so, until he has paid his due to the priest. Oh! would the true worshippers of living God, would learn of this giving lesson from Pagan neighbors, and enable the Church to send out more laborers into the vineyard of the Lord, even this great vineyard of China.

After having spent a week in Japan, we were again on the bosom of the deep; but it was not long before we reached our final destination. It was quite dark one evening when we were steaming up the river of Shanghai, and I felt as I were a stranger to the land that gave me birth.

The language of this people is entirely different from that of my mother tongue; hence I am just as much a stranger to these natives as I have been in America or Europe. As soon as our good ship ("Yokohama Maru") landed, Dr. Park and I rapidly get off, and making our way to Dr. J.W. Lambuth's house, where we spent the night. If it was not for Dr. Park's proficiency in Chinese language, we might have to run all over the settlement before we could get to Dr. Lambuth's.

At present, I am teaching English and studying Chinese in Soochow. Soochow is the capital of Kiangsu province, which is an interior city, but only eighty miles from Shanghai above the canal. This city is surrounded by a brick wall which is 12 miles in circumference, 25 feet in height, and 50 feet thick at the base.

The natives are very fond of Soochow, because it is considered to be one of the finest literary cities in the empire. Beside the literary attainment, it also produces some of the best silk and satin for Chinese market.

The population of the city is about two thousands, and nearly all of the houses are small and low, and none of them has more than two story in height. The streets are exceedingly narrow, some of them are not wider than six feet, and they are badly kept. There are no police here to keep public order, except a few watchmen who go from street to street during the late hours in the night to keep the thieves away. And as they do not want to catch them, they beat their gongs, rattle their drums and blow their horns to let the thieves know that they are coming.

Judging from what we have seen, our work in Soochow is quite promising. We have a hospital here where scores of patients could be seen daily within its walls. Beside hospital we have also two boarding schools, one for the boys, and the other for girls. In addition to the medical and educational work, we also have regular daily preaching. Brethren, pray for us and our work in this benighted land.[1]

Yours in Christ,
Charlie J. Soon
Soochow, China, Feb. 27th, 1886

Charlie's missionary teachers back in Tennessee and North Carolina were likely unprepared for the language obstacle that Charlie would face in Shanghai. He himself, in fact, seemed slightly taken aback by the revelation that the Chinese spoken in Shanghai was of an entirely different dialect than the Chinese he knew in Hainan. The fact that China is an enormous country with seven major dialects as mutually unintelligible to the speakers of each as German is from English was easy to forget. Charlie's unfamiliarity with the local language would be just one of the many factors that would contribute to his sense of alienation and loneliness in his first few years back in China.

According to the recollections of Charlie's good friend Bill Burke, Charlie lived with Dr. Park, his de facto supervisor and travel companion on the journey from America to China, for a few weeks; thereafter he moved in with a Chinese preacher whose experiences and circumstances were so remarkably akin to Charlie's that both men must have been startled upon introduction. The Chinese preacher's name was Dzau Tsz-zeh, otherwise known as C. K. (Charlie) Marshall.[2] Although now a Methodist preacher in Suzhou, as a child he was informally adopted and taken to the United States by Dr. D. C. Kelley, one of the first Methodist missionaries in Shanghai in the years before the U.S. Civil War. When the Civil War broke out, Dr. Kelley returned to America and served as a colonel in the Confederate Army and took C. K. along with him as a personal attendant, which, according to Burke, "threw him in a great deal among the Negro attendants of other Confederate officers." Although Marshall was in America for fourteen years, far longer than Charlie Soong, he too returned to China with a fluency in English and a "decided deep-South accent."[3]

The main purpose of Charlie's new living arrangements was to have C. K. teach him the local Shanghai dialect, but remembering his own native Hainanese Chinese dialect after living in the States for seven years was challenging enough for Charlie at times. Yung Wing, the first Chinese person to graduate from an American college, gave evidence two decades before that one's native language could easily be forgotten after an extended period living abroad in isolation from one's home country.[4] Charlie Soong was now experiencing this painful fact firsthand; in addition to relearning his native dialect, he now had to learn an entirely new one as well. English was the only common language between C. K. and Charlie, so it naturally served as their language of communication and of teaching. The two men got along well enough, it seemed, but conflicts inevitably arose. One particularly memorable argument between them broke out after Charlie politely corrected C. K.'s use of English while C. K was teaching him. It was not a welcome criticism.

"You, you upstart you!" C. K. cried. "Why you come pesterin' me wid dat Yankee talk. I bin' talkin' English 'fo you was ever born. Now go 'way and leave me 'lone." C. K.'s angry outburst directed at Charlie was not meant to be humorous, but Marshall's heavily accented English combined with his Southern drawl was enough to make Charlie burst out laughing.

Charlie may have been happy to finally be back in China, but his transition would not be free of turbulence. His first few years, in fact, would be full of enough trial and tribulation to justify a Job-like questioning of his faith. The first of these trials was in the form of his new supervisor, Dr. Young John Allen. Allen was born in Georgia in the 1830s and after having graduated from college, moved to Shanghai in 1860 to work as a missionary. He would spend nearly the next half-century there while becoming one of the shaping forces of the mission movement in China. Charlie's problems with the missionary leader had nothing to do with the incompetence or profligate tendencies on the part of Allen. Quite to the contrary, Allen was by all accounts a very serious and diligent man. Rather, the problems between Charlie and Allen lay in their radically different personalities, approaches, and backgrounds. Allen seemed to have many problems getting along with the missionaries sent to China, evidenced by the fact that many missionaries under his watch while Charlie was there applied for a transfer to Japan. In defense of Allen, he appears to have been an extremely bright and competent academic and bureaucrat, even if it was at the cost of others viewing him as a haughty, elitist, and professorial autocrat.

Part of the problem between Charlie and Allen was emblematic of a bigger rift in the missionary movement itself in China at the time. Ever since the days of Matteo Ricci, the famous Jesuit missionary in China in the late 1500s, a division existed in the mission movement as to how best approach the Chinese in order to most effectively bring about their eventual Christian conversion. As Ricci himself discovered, going the route of Jesus himself by dressing in rags and commingling with the poor was a technique destined to backfire among the extremely status-conscious Chinese; their Buddhist-influenced beliefs in fate dictated that poor people were poor because they deserved to be poor (as a result of transgressions from a previous life). The upper classes of Chinese society accorded no respect for such missionaries in Ricci's day, and even the majority of poor Chinese looked upon him with suspicion and derision (who but a raving lunatic, they surmised, would volunteer to be poor? they innocently asked).[5]

Ricci eventually discovered this for himself, and completely altered his approach to converting the Chinese by studiously courting Chinese mandarins and literati through the mastering of both the Chinese language and the Chinese classics, dressing like a Chinese scholar, and then tantalizing court officials and literati with his knowledge of Western science. He was so thorough in his approach, in fact, that he was eventually accepted by upper crust Chinese officials and literati as one of their own.

Ricci's strategy in China, as it evolved, became one of converting the upper classes with the belief that the lower classes would follow. This strategy was not as simple or clear cut as it sounded, however. One could only convert the upper classes by getting close to them, but one could only get close to them by essentially becoming one of them. Becoming a member of the upper class in China, however, necessitated largely cutting off all relations with members of the lower class—an action that most Christians would hardly call "Christian." The debate lingered among missionaries to China for centuries to come, and by the time Charlie Soong arrived in China, Dr. Allen was squarely in the camp of the old Jesuit Matteo Ricci.

Indeed, Dr. Allen was a diligent scholar and a prodigious translator of books and documents both into and out of Chinese. According to one author, he "gathered Chinese scholars around him to help mold his thoughts" into classical Chinese, the subset of Chinese language that was the exclusive domain of Chinese scholars and court officials (similar to the way Latin was used in the early and middle ages in Europe). Allen "then proceeded to write and translate on a prodigious scale." His books and pamphlets "contained facts of social and political as well as religious importance and were read by officials from the emperor on down." This was widely recognized among missionaries as taking the "educational" approach to missionary work in China. The Chinese government, in return for his tireless devotion to his translating work and his mastery of the Chinese language, "ranked Allen as a magistrate" and "his house bore the insignia of an official residence."[6]

Charlie's relationship with Dr. Allen was doomed before it even began. In a letter written just days before Charlie's arrival in China and dated January 12, 1886, Dr. Allen wrote back to the Mission Board in the United States that Charlie had no business working and mingling amongst the likes of him and his intellectual cohorts.

> ...There is yet one other item—Item 10—which I should like to refer to–to wit the salary of Mr. Soon. He will be here two days from now and I have no information as to how the Board expects to treat him. What is to be his status and pay. There is much that is embarrassing in this case. The boys and young men in our Anglo-*Chinese* college are far his superiors in that they are—the advanced ones—both English and Chinese scholars, and

can do and have done work here in the way of compo-
sition and translation that has won the encomiums of
our eldest and ablest missionaries in public conference
of missionaries when the work was presented and criti-
cized. And Soon will never become a Chinese scholar, at
best will only be a *denationalized* Chinaman, discontented
and unhappy unless he is located and paid far beyond
his deserts—and the consequence is I find none of our
brotherin willing to take him.[7]

There was talk in the United States of Charlie assuming a
university position in Shanghai, but, as with many bureaucracies,
good intra-organizational communication was lacking. Charlie
may have been promised a university position in Shanghai while
he was still in America, but the truth was he had absolutely no
business working amongst Chinese scholars and literati who had
spent their whole lives studying classical Chinese, a language so
difficult that even the Chinese themselves, with the exception of
a tiny few intellectual elite, never learn it. As harsh as Dr. Allen's
words seemed on paper, they were likely true. No schools or acad-
emies were likely to want Charlie working for them with his limited background as a scholar. He may have had experience living
in two cultures, but to call him a scholar after a four-year cram
session in America was exaggerating more than a bit. He would
never be welcomed into the snobbishly elite world of Chinese
scholars and academics who'd had their noses firmly parked between the pages of a book since the day they were born.

After six months in China Charlie still had no opportunity to
return home to Hainan for a visit with his parents and family, but
he was nonetheless enthusiastic in a letter written to the *Raleigh
Christian Advocate* about the possibility of Soochow (Suzhou)

being the "evangelical center" of the Methodist Church in the province and he hoped that God would "hasten the time when we will be able to send faithful men and women from this place… to the millions in other parts of China."[8] In a personal letter written soon afterwards to someone identified only as "my dearest Friend," however, Charlie is much more forthcoming. It is clear that his reverse culture shock is in full swing and his homesickness for America is at fever pitch. He also mentions for the first time his discontent with his current work situation.

My dearest friend:

Your kind and highly appreciated letter of April the 30th came last Saturday (12th) and I was exceedingly pleased and glad to hear from you. This is a second letter I received from you since my arrival in China. Please accept my grateful appreciation for both of them. It is a matter of delight to know those shoes and tea have reached their intended destination and were so highly prized by the receiver.

Yes, the teas was intended for my most excellent friend, Mr. James Southgate of Durham…

…Yes, I am walking once more in the land that gave me birth, but it is far from being a homelike place to me. I felt more homelike in America than I do in China.

No, I haven't been to see my parents as yet. Dr. Allen said I may go during the coming Chinese new year and not before then. I am very much displeased with this sort of authority; but I must bear it patiently. If I were to take a rash action the people at home might not fail to understand the nature of the case, and they (my Durham friends especially) might think that I am an unloyal

Methodist and a law breaker, so I have kept as silent as
a mouse. But when the fullness of time has come, I will
shake off all the assuming authority of the present Supt.
in spite of all his protestation, assuming authority, and
the detestation of native ministry. The great "Ch(m)
ogul" (?) was the man that wanted to dismiss all the native ministers from preaching about a year ago. And he
is the man that ignores my privileges and equality which
I am entitled to. I don't like to work under him—I will
apply for transmission to Japan.

If I go home at all, I want to go sometime in next
spring, for toward and during the Chinese New Year, the
Chinese are very bad on the coast and on the island of
Hainan.

Intelligence reached us last Saturday (12ᵗʰ) that the
Board has decided to establish a mission operation in
Japan. To which field the following gentlemen have
been appointed to work viz.: Dr. J.W. Lambuth, Dr. W.R.
Lambuth (son of J.W.L) and Dr. Dukes. None of these mis-
sionaries could stand the "one man power' at Shanghai.

As I am not feeling well this afternoon, I will this letter before it is half done.

Will write you again and longer in some other time.
Love to all.⁹

Yours ever truly,
Charlie

The smattering of remaining letters that would trickle into
North Carolina from Charlie during 1886 would be written
mostly to the *Raleigh Christian Advocate*, the mouthpiece for the

Methodist church in North Carolina. Although largely imper-
sonal in nature and content, they do describe the situation that
Charlie faced in China when he first arrived. In August Charlie
would write yet another letter to the newspaper highlighting his
complaints about the perpetual status quo of affairs in China
that seems to paralyze the country, and its seeming inability to
progress.

> Generations after generations have passed and gone,
> but scarcely any change of importance has taken place in
> this great empire... Should anyone living in China desire
> to obtain an accurate knowledge of the ancient habits,
> customs, and practices of this people; he does not need to
> go to any book or manuscript to find out what they were;
> Because the old China is the old China still. The Chinese
> today are doing precisely what their ancestors did years
> ago. They don't want any new things in their country, all
> they care to do is maintain they're ancestral habits...[10]

Charlie, of course, could not help but compare China to
America and the West, and the comparisons were rarely flatter-
ing to China. He even goes so far as to praise the European invasions of China as the only reliable agents of change in China.

> Thus far, China has not voluntarily moved a foot to-
> ward Western civilization and improvement, except that
> which has been done by compulsion of treaty and for fear
> of foreign encroachment. If it had not been for the French
> and English cannons which thundered on these shores
> from time to time, China to-day would be exactly where
> she was when her Confucian civilization was dated...

He also writes of a mob of Chinese recently returned from the United States who attacked local missionaries out of revenge for their maltreatment in the United States. They "burned down the dwellings and the Chapels of the Missionaries" and the missionaries had to escape "for the safety of their lives." It was also unfortunate, Charlie wrote, that "two of the ringleaders of the outrage upon the Chinese in the United States were ministers of the Gospel." Charlie feared that the "evil deed of these so called ministers…has done much to the prejudice of missionary operations and the cause of Christ" in China.

Recent incidents of child abduction in and around Soochow were also discussed by Charlie, and seemed to have been difficult for him to forget. The account Charlie provides is as shocking as it is heartbreaking; it also provides brief insight into the Chinese legal and justice system at the time.

There has been a family in Soochow which consisted of two sons and mater-familias, who made their life-vocation the stealing of children and sold them to some wealthy families of the neighboring cities as domestic slaves. One of these thieves has stolen fourteen children from some unfortunate parents of this city and has sold them for money. But the thief has been caught and was arrested and sentenced to capital punishment by the Chief Magistrate. The mode of punishment of this kind of crime is to imprison the prisoner in a little wooden cage and make him abstain from food. The thief is dead. The other two will also be arrested and will be treated likewise, sharing a similar fate.

Overall, the only thing predictable about Charlie's reentry into the land of his birth was its unpredictability. Charlie himself was a mixed bag of emotions regarding his return to China. The excitement he felt one day, perhaps owing to some work related achievement, could be quickly flushed away by the homesickness or loneliness that would wash over him the next. Regardless, he maintained a steadiness of purpose and an indefatigable spirit that would eventually pay off, although not in ways that he likely ever imagined.

CHAPTER 8

FRIENDS OLD AND NEW

───ᴏᴇᴇᴏ───

FOREIGNERS OFTEN ROMANTICALLY REFERRED TO Shanghai in the late nineteenth and early twentieth century as "the Paris of the East," for the city was indeed more similar in appearance to its European namesake than it was to other Chinese cities. However, the influx of so much money and so many wealthy foreign businessmen, who usually arrived in China unattached, meant that life in Shanghai often took on a life of its own, often stretching far beyond the limits of conventional propriety. While no city is without its share of crime and vice, certain parts of Shanghai at the time of Charlie's arrival there elevated the arts of hedonism and debauchery to levels that China had perhaps never known before.

Opium use in Shanghai in the late nineteenth century was so widespread that nearly one thousand five-hundred opium houses were reported to be in operation in the port city. The smell of opium smoke so permeated the air that foreigners visiting Shanghai just once would never forget the smell. One foreign journalist visiting China in the late nineteenth century commented that although Chinese bureaucrats frequently crafted edicts and laws designed to curb the opium problem, they were merely for show since the great majority of them were "drawn up by Chinese philanthropists over a quiet pipe of opium, signed by opium-smoking officials, whose revenues are derived from poppy, and posted near fields of poppy…"[1]

Gambling too was an activity with no shortage of enthusiasts in Shanghai, and was most famously pursued by wealthy foreigners at the illustrious Shanghai Race Club. Other more humble but far more widespread forms of gambling allowed even the poorest of Shanghai's poor to entertain themselves. Also high on the list of Shanghai's tourist attractions was, not surprisingly, prostitution. In addition to young Chinese women arriving from various parts of China to work in the industry, a thriving business in "light ladies"—Caucasian women brought from overseas (always introduced as American, regardless of what country they were from) for the specific purpose of serving as "escorts" to any upper-class Shanghai residents that could afford their services. At one point, Japanese ships sailing from the U.S. came to be jokingly referred to as "the girl ships." Amongst the attributes that contributed to their fame was the fact that many of the women passengers were supposedly permitted to board without as much a penny in their purse. They were, however, expected to pay for their ticket at the end of the voyage, by which time they usually had acquired the necessary funds to purchase their ticket.[2]

The accumulation of so much vice in Shanghai has been attributed to various causes. "Volumes of idle moments" and "lack of any effective local public opinion to compel the maintenance of social standards" were identified by some as the chief culprits, and the cheap labor provided by local Chinese only added to the excess of leisure time that became the trademark of so many foreign businessmen. "There was never much left for the foreign 'masters' to do," wrote one observer," that could not be "put off until tomorrow." This, in turn, led to a leisurely work day that meant, "business hours were ten to three, with two hours off for tiffin (breakfast or lunch)."[3]

Into such a bizarre and foreign world Charlie Soong was thrust his first year in China, and rarely a day passed when the strangeness and unfamiliarity of the land of his birth did not directly appeal to his sense of irony. If temptation was ever incarnate, it was indeed in late nineteenth century Shanghai. From its lax morals to its watered down Chinese identity, there was little that was pure about it. Despite this, Charlie seemed to have had little trouble navigating the vices of Shanghai. By all accounts he took his job as a missionary as seriously as any of his cohorts, and performed all duties with a diligence and sincerity that would become his hallmarks later in life.

Eventually Charlie's local language lessons concluded and he was assigned to a mission school in the vicinity of Shanghai (Kunshan) sometime in late 1886. Although it was a job far removed from the prestigious professorship that was so gloriously reported in North Carolina newspapers to have been waiting for him in China, he immersed himself in his new role as a teacher of young Chinese students at a recently opened mission school. Dr. Hu Shi, a former student of Charlie's, as well as a later preeminent Chinese scholar and diplomat, recalled Soong's first day as a teacher during a speech later given at Duke University. "One day a short, stocky man, rather ugly, appeared on the teacher's platform. They (the students) immediately began to laugh at him and created such a hullabaloo that Hu thought the teacher would leave the room for shame. Instead, Charles Soong waited for the hubbub to subside, and then he opened his books and began to talk." Hu later went on to praise Charlie as "the most popular teacher at the school."[4]

It took Charlie several years to re-adapt to China after his arrival in Shanghai in 1886, but it could easily be argued that his adaptation was never really complete. For the remainder of his life in China, he not only retained many of the habits and ways of thinking he acquired in America, but they became somewhat of a calling card for him. Charlie's love of American food, the frank and candid manner in which he dealt with friends and business associates alike, and his passion for Christianity and American education (especially the education of women) were as synonymous with Charlie Soong in Shanghai as Shanghai was with commerce. The fact that, in later years, he fit in just as well, perhaps even better, at a gathering of American businessmen or missionaries as he did with a roomful of Chinese made him a unique creature in Shanghai, but just as assuredly it could also make him feel a perpetual outsider.

During the five years after his initial arrival in Shanghai, Charlie was more concerned with being a good missionary than being any sort of revolutionary. Family concerns were also weighing heavily upon his heart at the time. A letter written back to Mr. Southgate in Durham, North Carolina, reveals, among other things, that one of his greatest desires was fulfilled when he was finally given the opportunity to visit his parents in Hainan.

Soochow, China
Oct. 7, 1886

My dear Mr. Southgate,
Your nice letter of Aug. 1st has been received a few days since. Glad to hear from you and please to get such an elegant letter but sorry to learn that you had trouble with your sore foot and confinement. However, I trust

that you are entirely well by this. Bishop Wilson arrived in Shanghai a week ago last Tuesday, and has gone to Peking on a speculating tour. The bishop may get back to Shanghai toward the last of this month, but our annual meeting will not take place until the middle of November. The weather is quite pleasant in this part of the country now. This is a Thursday and I have just returned from our weekly prayer meeting. The Southern Presbyterian missionaries are now having their annual meeting in this city. Dr. W.H. Park of our mission has gone to Japan to get marry and will back to his duty on the 20th. By the way, I have succeeded in paying my folks a visit since I wrote you. All the members of my family are well. They were very glad to see me though none could recognized my person. I had a warm reception from them. At present there is a little war going on between the natives of Hainan and imperial troops. I thought I could have a taste of gun powder while on my way to Hainan but the war was too far from my home to see any fun. The native Roman Catholic Christians in Ichang have given a great deal of trouble to the local mandarins and people; but alas, they only brought destruction upon themselves.

Please remember me kindly to all. I shall write you a longer letter when I have more news to give.[5]

Goodbye
Yours truly
Charlie Soon

In addition to providing evidence that Charlie finally succeeded in paying his parents a visit in Hainan, the brief mention of the "Roman Catholic Christians" by Charlie is a reminder of the often bitter and always ironic conflict between various sects of Christianity and their missions in China. His ever-so-slight disparagement of the local Catholic mission in Hainan hints that the rivalry between the different branches of Christianity in Asia was as real as ever, although not as intense as centuries prior when missionaries from competing branches of Christianity were occasionally quite literally at each other's throats.

It was sometime in January 1887, right around the time of his one-year anniversary in China, that Charlie learned of a tragedy that had recently occurred back in Durham and, for a brief time anyway, reawakened his longing for days past in North Carolina. In a letter to Mr. Southgate in Durham, the sorrow Charlie expressed over the death of his dear friend, Annie Southgate, was so genuine and so timeless that it is still capable of arousing emotion. In the letter Charlie also provides details of his current work assignment.

Kuensan, Feb. 4, 1887

My dear Mr. Southgate,

It is a matter of great sorrow to learn the death of Miss Annie; though on the contrary do rejoice to know that she is happier in heaven than could possibly be on earth. And no doubt all things work for good to them that love God. May god comfort you all and sustain you with his tender love and grace; and finally when our work is done in this life we may all meet her on that happy shore where there is no parting.

Miss Annie was one of my best friends. Her Christian example is worthy of attention. When left America I had no idea of such event would have occured so soon, and that we are not permitted to meet again on this side of Jordan. O, this is sad to think of. The sweetest flower God has plucked off and took away from us; but that very identical flower is blooming in the garden of God in Heaven. Happy art thou who sleeps in the Lord. And thrice happy art thou who being translated from earthly sorrow to heavenly joy. May God keep us from sin and weakness and finally translate us to his home where we will meet all our friends and loved ones and to live with Christ forever.

I have begun to preach in this dialect though not as fluently as I would like to and will be after a while. The Chinese New Year has just passed, But the holiday is not yet over. The Chinese have no sabbaths during the year, and when they do have it, they extend to two or three weeks. Our school (day) will be opened on the 16th of this moon or Feb. 8th. Last year we had 12 pupils but the coming session we expect to have twice as many.

Kuensan is a wall city of 4 miles in circumference. It has a population of 300,000 including the suburbs. At present, we have three different denominations represented here besides the various sects of heathen religions. We, the Southern Methodist, the Southern Baptist, the French Catholic, the Buddhist, the Taoist, & the Mohamedan. The Northern Presbyterian used to be here, but as they had no house of their own and the landlord turned them out from the house they did stay in, so they were compelled to move to another place.

Please pray for me and work. May God give us abundance of success in the coming year and that we may experience more deeply of his love to usward.

Give my love to all.

I shall be glad to hear from you at any time.

I beg to remain yours most gratefully,[6]

Charlie,
C.J. Soong
Cfo. Rev. C.F. Reid,
Shanghai, China.

In the letter Charlie highlighted the various branches of Christianity represented by the missionaries in China, including the Methodists, Baptists, Catholics, and Presbyterians. Local Buddhist, Taoist, and Muslim sects, he emphasized, were also present in the area. More importantly, he reiterated the difficulties associated with learning and speaking the local dialect. Even after a year of living in Shanghai, it is clear that Charlie was still struggling to fit in and that the language barriers associated with conducting missionary work in China were far more formidable than either he or his supervisors ever suspected. The fact that a useful and effective translation system for transcribing Chinese sounds into English (hence the varied and often confusing spellings of places like Suzhou, which is sometimes seen as *Soochow* or *Suchow,* and Kunshan, which is often spelled as *Kuensan* or *Kwensan*), had yet to be invented didn't make things any easier for him when working across cultures.

Charlie Soong may have been Chinese, but for all practical purposes he was an expat living in his own country. For several years after moving to China, the food, the language, the local customs, and the local religions were all as foreign to him as they were to any of his American missionary friends. He was arguably more American in his tastes and attitudes than Chinese at this point in his life, and likely wondered if he could ever fully re-adapt to China. He had no taste for Chinese food, a sin considered unforgivable and unfathomable to most Chinese, and his speech was as foreign to the residents of Shanghai as German or Greek; when he did manage to learn the local Shanghai dialect, it was almost certainly spoken with a heavy accent that marked him as a "foreigner" whenever he was amongst the local Chinese population.

It had been nearly two years since Charlie arrived in China, and old familiar faces were a rare sight when Vanderbilt class-mate William Burke, the practical joker who Charlie met in his college dormitory back in 1882, arrived in Shanghai in 1887 to work as a missionary. It was at the annual Methodist missionary conference in Shanghai, held immediately after Burke's arrival, that the two were unexpectedly reunited. Neither recognized the other upon first glance, since both men had changed in appearance since their college days. Charlie was especially difficult to recognize since "his face was much fuller" and he was wearing his "long Chinese gown and a black silk skullcap." It was Burke who finally recognized Charlie.

"Well, sakes alive, Charlie, it's mighty good to see you again! It's been over two years!" he exclaimed.[7]

"I'm glad to see you too, Bill!...I didn't know you with that beard."

"Well, I didn't know you in that Chinese getup of yours either," Burke laughed.

As soon as the conference concluded, Burke was back at Charlie's house reminiscing and learning all about Charlie's life in China since his arrival there two years prior. Not surprisingly, the conversation soon turned into a discussion about women and dating. More pertinently, it evolved into a brief recount of Charlie's recent dating experiences in China. One woefully awkward experience that Charlie relayed to Burke illustrated the difficulties he faced transitioning back to life in China. It took place not long after he had arrived in China and came into the acquaintance of a young schoolteacher in Nansiang at the Methodist mission school there. It's not known exactly how Charlie became acquainted with the young lady, or if she was Chinese or American, but in the usual directness that character- ized Charlie and his approach to things, he went directly to the principal of the mission school and asked permission to call on the new apple of his eye.

Miss Lockie Rankin, the principal of the school, was not a woman likely proficient in the art of courtship, be it of the American or Chinese variety.[8] She was chosen for mission work in China because she was "a single woman well versed in ancient and modern languages." As a further obstacle for Charlie, the Southern custom of "calling on" young ladies as a form of court- ship was yet another American custom that had not yet taken root in China. Indeed, proper courtship rituals in China at the time usually didn't even involve an introduction between the bachelor and bachelorette. Rather, a matchmaker was typically used to connect an available bachelor with available bachelorettes, and it was the parents, not the children, who decided whom their children were matched with.

Charlie's request to Miss Rankin to call on the young teacher was denied before he even finished getting the words out of his mouth. Not only that, Miss Rankin took the extra step of or- dering the teacher that was the object of Charlie's affections be sequestered in her room until Charlie "was well out of town." Reeling from the insult, Charlie realized once and for all that many of the "professional" missionaries in Shanghai were a completely separate breed from his Methodist friends and mentors back in North Carolina, whose generosity, kindness, and hospitality had transformed his very existence. It wasn't just the missionaries that would lead to difficulties in Charlie's transition back into Chinese life, however. It would also be the Chinese themselves who would see Charlie not as one of them, but as a sort of Chinese-American mutt who looked as out of place on the streets of China as any other foreigner. Charlie had no way of knowing it, but it was this distinct inability to fit in in China and his often distinctly Western tastes that, combined with the revival of his good old-fashioned lucky streak, would help to bring about his sudden and unexpected courtship with a most unusual Chinese girl and bring his lonely bachelorhood to an end.

In a letter to the *Raleigh Christian Advocate* written just after his reunion with Burke, Charlie reiterated that his missionary commitment was still strong. More importantly, however, he revealed something of a more personal nature that would have a profound impact on the rest of his life.

> *Dear Bro. Reid:* It is the time for me to break my long silence. It has been nearly a year since I wrote you, and I suppose you have come to the conclusion that I have forgotten the old good Christian Advocate. No, no. I haven't forgotten it, but on the contrary, I thought a great deal of it, and quite often.
>
> Well, the good Lord has been very gracious to us, and we feel very grateful to Him. The outlook is very promising. The spirit of the Lord is rapidly making his

way into the hearts of His benighted people. We pray and hope that the Lord will give us many souls during this year for Christ.

Our China Mission Conference has met and closed. No change was made as to our appointments. Every man returned to his own charge. I returned to Kwensau (Kunshan) for another year. By the grace and help of God, I hope to do better and more work for my Savior than I ever did before.

Our hospital for women in Suchow is completed. But the physician in charge, Dr. Philips, is sick in Shanghai.

Our new brick church in the English concession at Shanghai is receiving its last finishing touch.

China is about to turn over another new leaf. She has all sorts of plans and schemes on hand. The government is contemplating building a long railway from Peking to Canton as a passenger train, and another railroad is to be constructed in the island of Formosa for carrying imperial troops up and down the wilderness to subjugate the wild tribe of that island.

Well, I shall come to a close, but before I do so, I must tell you I am different from what I used to be—I am married, The ceremony was performed by Rev. C.F. Reid of our Mission.[9]

Yours affectionately,
C.J. Soon.
Kwensaw, China, Nov. 4th, '87.

Soon after arriving in Shanghai, Charlie realized that finding a wife was going to be more difficult than he anticipated. The

dearth of Western woman, not to mention the overwhelmingly
negative sentiments still attached to interracial marriages at the
time, meant that marrying an American was highly unlikely. By
the same token, the prospect of marrying a local girl was likely to
pose challenges equally as insurmountable. The overwhelming
majority of them were not Christian, a fact likely to not sit well
with Charlie. In addition, most local Chinese women were not
likely to be educated, another factor that could have hindered
Charlie's ability to identify with them. Indeed, the chances of
Charlie finding a suitable and appropriate mate in Shanghai
were slim. And then came along Miss Ni Kwei-tseng.

Charlie wasn't directly introduced to Miss Ni, nor did he
actively pursue her the way he might have done in America by
going straight to her parents to ask permission to court her.
Charlie had finally learned his lesson and proved it this time by
letting his old friend from Boston, C. S. New, play matchmaker
for him. Both of his old Boston comrades, New and Wen, had
moved to Shanghai after moving back from America. Not surprisingly, it wasn't long after Charlie's arrival in Shanghai that he
bumped into C. S. New one day while strolling down the street.
Of course, the two old friends reconnected and Charlie eventually informed New of his recent streak of bad luck in the dating
department. Charlie's timing couldn't have been more perfect.
New had just recently married a local girl.

And she had a sister.

Miss Ni was nineteen when Charlie met her. In appearance,
she kept her jet black hair tightly pulled back. Her oval face,
thin lips, and almond eyes likely never met with much in the
way of makeup given her parents' strict religious background.
Prominent crescent moon eyebrows adorned her eyes and a flat,
wide nose graced a face that while plain was indicative of the

plain and simple life she was used to living. New described Miss Ni's background to Charlie, and the more he spoke, the more Charlie listened. First and foremost, she was Christian. Miss Ni was not just any ordinary Christian, however. She was, if there is such a thing, a member of the Christian royalty in China. She was descended from a long line of Christians that traced their family heritage back three centuries to Hsu Kwang Chi, a Ming Dynasty prime minister who was personally converted to Christianity by Matteo Ricci, the Jesuit scholar-missionary who lived in China during the late 1500s and early 1600s. Miss Ni's mother, however, in what likely led to a family scandal of sorts in the staunch Catholic Chinese family, converted to Protestantism when she married her husband (who was converted by the London Missionary Society in Shanghai) a few decades before Charlie's arrival in Shanghai.

If Miss Ni's Christianity was not enough to throw Charlie over the moon, New went on to describe another aspect of the unusual young debutante from the suburbs of Shanghai. The fact that Miss Ni had any education at all was unusual in a country that was famous for the idiom *zhong nan qing nu*, the cultural dictum mandating that boys are to be highly regarded and girls are not. Traditionally, this idiom extended to the realm of education in China, as well, where girls were typically ignored. Miss Ni's parents couldn't seem to pry her from her books when she was a child, however, and all attempts to interest her in more "feminine" pursuits apparently failed. Consequently, her open-minded parents, with the help of local mission schools, enrolled her in schooling far beyond what any typical Chinese girl would receive. Miss Ni's obsession with learning was proof enough to her parents that no matter how hard they tried to find her a marriage partner, they would likely never succeed since most

Chinese men would never marry a highly educated woman. In addition, Miss Ni was "afflicted" with a physical condition that should have guaranteed her lifelong status as a bachelorette in China; it even rendered her somewhat of the ugly duckling in her own family. The embarrassing affliction was that Miss Ni's feet were uncommonly large.

In reality, Miss Ni's feet were quite normal, but in a culture obsessed with the ancient practice of foot binding, they were anything but. Miss Ni's own mother and two older sisters had all endured the excruciating process of foot binding at a young age, and had to bear the painful deformation for the rest of their lives, but when her parents attempted to bind her feet when she was young, she took to it rather badly and they eventually gave up. Her mother was herself growing to be less and less a fan of the bizarre Chinese custom after a particularly harrowing and painful experience; a band of soldiers had attacked her village during the Taiping Rebellion and forced her and her family to flee to a neighboring town. Every step of the journey on her bound feet was, not surprisingly, an exercise in pure agony, which helped harden her opposition to the well-entrenched custom. When Miss Ni's parents resigned themselves to the decision not to bind their youngest daughters' feet, they also resigned themselves even more to the likelihood that she, unlike her two sisters, would never marry. Ironically, however, the traits that rendered her so undesirable in Chinese culture only made her all the more attractive to Charlie Soong.[10]

With the help of New and his matchmaking skills, it wasn't long before Charlie was introduced to both Miss Ni and her parents. When Charlie finally did meet her, all of his expectations must have been fully realized, for on October 8, 1887, the following notice appeared on the other side of the world in the

Morning Star in Wilmington, which, in turn, quoted an article from a local Durham newspaper.

> The *Tobacco Plant* says: "Rev. Charlie J. Soon will be married to Miss Mamie Nei, at Shanghai, China on the 4th day of the Chinese 9th moon. Those who can figure out when that is are cordially invited to be present."[11]

Charlie had not forgotten his old North Carolina friends, and he proved it by inviting them to his wedding. North Carolina may have been oceans away, but it was still held closely in the heart of Charlie Soong.

While Charlie was busy transitioning to missionary life and married life in Shanghai in the late 1880s, Sun Yat-sen was busy settling into life in Hong Kong. While he seems to have been studiously engaged in his medical studies at the Hong Kong College of Medicine for Chinese, he also frequently found time to sit around with friends and discuss and debate current events in China. Known collectively and somewhat romantically in Chinese history as the Four Bandits, the group consisted of Sun Yat-sen and three of his closest friends.[12] Like many discontented citizens of China at the time, their desire to overthrow the Qing was rooted not only in their intense hatred of the Manchus, but in the widespread dissatisfaction and anger that everyday Chinese felt as they watched their once-proud nation slowly crumble in the face of repeated foreign invasions under ever-increasingly incompetent leadership.

The hatred that the so-called Four Bandits harbored toward the Manchu leadership was not uncommon in China in the nineteenth century, for the Manchus had long been considered invaders in the eyes of the Chinese. Now that Chinese society was beginning to self-destruct, all eyes frequently turned toward the Manchu emperor and the power hungry dowager empress Cixi as the source of all blame. In fact, nearly all of the suffering that cropped up in nineteenth century China, and there was plenty to go around, was blamed on ineffective Manchu leadership.

From the disastrous confrontations with the British that led to the humiliating Opium Wars to the Taiping Rebellion that had nearly brought down the entire dynasty thirty years before, the eyes of most Chinese fell squarely on the shoulders of the leadership in Beijing when it came to casting blame. On one level, the Four Bandits, one of whom was from Sun's hometown of Cuiheng, were nothing more than a group of college buddies who regularly sat around engaging in figurative dorm room bull sessions little different from the ones that occur every day on every college campus around the world. On a deeper level, however, the opportunity and support from friends that Sun received at this crucial time in his life served as the seeds of his future revolutionary activities. Sun was studying to be a doctor, and had things turned out differently career-wise for him, he may have been just another wealthy and well-fed Western-trained physician who made financial donations to revolutionary causes from afar while reminiscing about his own "radical" college days discussing revolution with old classmates. This scenario, however, would never come to pass, and Sun's time with the Four Bandits would be more relevant and influential than anyone could have ever known.

CHAPTER 9

BREAKING AWAY

⸺⸘⸙⸺

CHARLIE SOONG'S RE-TRANSPLANTATION BACK TO China seemed to be going well enough a few years in. He was settled into his mission job and he was married at last. Eventually, however, cracks began appearing in the missionary zeal that had taken root so thoroughly and resolutely in Charlie's character. Not surprisingly, the first of these cracks was apparently brought on by the forceful leadership style of his supervisor, Dr. Allen. In a previous letter to his friend in Durham, Charlie had mentioned that in regards to his supervisors he was "very much displeased with their sort of authority" and that he didn't "like to work under" them, but that he had to keep "as silent as a mouse" in order to preserve his integrity in the eyes of his "Durham friends." When the time was right, however, Charlie promised to "shake off all the assuming authority" and "apply for transmission to Japan."

Charlie never did get around to applying for a transfer to Japan, but the discontent that surfaced at this time in his life proved more than just a passing phase. Although he was diligent and disciplined in his missionary work and his letters to the *Raleigh Christian Advocate* conveyed nothing but enthusiasm and confidence, a conversation with his friend Burke betrayed deeper feelings of discontent brewing under the surface, perhaps partially indicative of a sense of homesickness in Charlie and a belief that the United States, not China, was his true home. It is entirely possible that in his first year or two in China Charlie had high hopes of returning to North Carolina. He did, after all, frequently refer to Durham, North Carolina, as his "home" in letters, and most other missionaries sent from the United States eventually returned home, if only for a visit. Perhaps Charlie just assumed the same would be true of him. Such would not be the case, however. Feeling neither fully Chinese nor fully American, Charlie's identity now was still as malleable as the North Carolina clay upon which he once trod as a result of his inability to really fit in amongst local Shanghai residents. The discussion with William Burke during his second visit to Kunshan (昆山) to see Charlie during the Chinese New Year holiday of 1888 is as humorous as it is revelatory.

The visit began with Burke's arrival by boat in Kunshan. A crowd gathered at the docks in Kunshan as locals ogled the new foreigner in their midst. Foreigners were not yet a common sight in Kunshan, so Burke's arrival was somewhat of a spectacle, especially given that he was a very large-framed man. Charlie greeted Burke, and afterwards a local shouted something in Chinese that Charlie immediately translated. "Two foreign devils. A giant and a dwarf."[1]

"Do you see, Bill?" Charlie said. "The foreigners treat me like a Chinese and here you witness a Chinese saying I am a foreigner." Charlie was only half-joking. As the two men walked along the street to Charlie's house, a crowd followed. It being Chinese New Year, there were also fireworks exploding in abundance.

"Not a welcome for you, Bill," Charlie jokingly apologized, telling Burke that it was "for the god of wealth" instead.

Upon returning to Charlie's humble home, a "two-story, tile roof house nestled in a line of identical buildings," Charlie lit an oil stove for heat, a small luxury for local Chinese, and Burke noticed paper covering the cracks around all the windows. "I can never be Chinese enough to want to sit in a cold room with all my outdoor clothes on," Charlie quipped, subtly bringing to the surface again the voids in his Chinese identity as a result of living in America so long. Indeed, there were a lot of situations in which Charlie found himself in China where he could "never be Chinese enough," and one of them included being treated like a native preacher. His bubbling discontent overflowed for the first time in the company of friends when he disclosed to Burke his current emotional state regarding his work as a missionary.[2]

"Sometimes I think I could do more for my people if I were free of the mission, Bill," Charlie said. "You know the way I feel about the material and spiritual burdens under which I labor in the mission."[3] Charlie was referring to his love of the work he was doing in contrast to the low salary and the unequal treatment he received because of what he considered his unfair classification as a "native preacher," especially since "he was in as responsible a position as some of the foreign missionaries." Ten dollars a month barely covered expenses for him and his wife. It was painfully obvious that such a stipend would be woefully insufficient when they decided to have children.

"But please believe me, Bill. If I do happen to leave the mission, it will never mean my giving up of preaching Christ and Him crucified. I will continue to work as much as I can for the mission always."

It is apparent that leaving the Methodist mission was certainly not a decision taken lightly by Charlie. It is easy to overlook the tremendous risk that accompanied the decision, but it was one pregnant with consequence. If things did not work out, Charlie's predicament in Shanghai may have quickly gone from bad to worse. Once he made the decision, there was no turning back, and he would no longer enjoy the support of the mission and the network of friends that he had built up ever since washing up upon the shores of North Carolina. While his inability to get along well with the upper echelon of the Methodist mission in Shanghai certainly contributed to his discontent, it appears that practical concerns motivated Charlie to leave the mission even more.

Despite Charlie's statements about leaving the mission earlier, his departure from it does not appear to have been conducted in any sort of rash manner. Rather, it was a gradual process that evolved over a number of years and seems to have begun when he found a part-time job in Shanghai to supplement his mission work. It may have been exhausting at times, but he was lucky in the fact that he probably could not have found a job more suitable to his skills and experience than the one he found—selling bibles for the American Bible Society.

The American Bible Society, a New York-based organization established in 1816 (and still in existence today), was established, in its own words, in order to "deliver God's Word to hard-to-reach places" and "bring God's word to cultural channels where the Bible lacks a strong voice." The main mission of the ABS was to provide a Bible to anyone in the world who wanted one, and presumably to provide them even if they didn't. Far from being some tiny missionary outfit operating out of a basement in some New York alley, the American Bible Society was about as prestigious as such a religious institution could get in the nineteenth century. Among its presidents in the decades before Charlie began working for them was the likes of John Jay, the first chief justice of the United States, and Richard Varick, a former mayor of New York City.[4]

With the ever-increasing number of American missionaries pouring into China in the second half of the nineteenth century, it was only natural that the demand for bibles should also increase in China. When it did, the American Bible Society, and now Charlie Soong, were there to meet the demand. As Charlie discovered, however, there was more than meets the eye to the supposedly simple idea of selling bibles to the Chinese masses. As with much in China at the time, the situation was slightly more complicated than it seemed.

All the talk of revolution in China in nineteenth century was not limited to politics and government. A no less relevant topic of revolutionary debate was also beginning to rage in the field of education. More specifically, a movement was afoot amongst Chinese intellectuals to radically alter the Chinese language. Simply stated, language in China has always been a complicated affair, but reading and writing Chinese were skills never meant for everyone. The language of highly educated Chinese (always a tiny fraction of the Chinese population at large) used in all books and literature was known as classical Chinese. Radically different in both content and appearance from the language that most Chinese spoke on an everyday basis, the existence and use of classical Chinese essentially guaranteed that the great majority of Chinese could never read books, and it denied most Chinese people access to their own culture's greatest literary, political, and scientific works in the same way that Latin did in medieval Europe. Some have argued that classical Chinese served as a subtle form of class control in China for centuries that weighed upon social class mobility in Chinese society like a boulder; by the end of the nineteenth century Chinese intellectual radicals had had enough.

The printing of books and manuscripts using the vernacular language (and characters) became increasingly common in China as the twentieth century approached, and an ever-increasing demand for vernacular books fed right into the trend. It is unknown just how much Charlie thought in advance about the economics of the publishing business in China and the momentous opportunity that the vernacular movement was about to create when he got into the business of selling bibles for the American Bible Society. Regardless, the economics of publishing and printing became something very familiar to him afterwards, so that he would soon make another momentous decision that would again profoundly alter the course of his life: he would go from selling bibles to printing them.

It has been said that Charlie's bible printing business was possible because of his experience working in a printing shop in Wilmington and because Julian Carr provided Charlie with a generous capital injection. No substantial evidence to support either of these assertions exists, however.[5] A more likely explanation for Charlie's printing business savvy was his possible acquaintance with a man known as Wang Tao (王韜), a well-known resident of Shanghai who, although a generation older than Charlie, could not have been more similar in terms of background and life experience. More importantly for Charlie, however, Wang Tao was not only somewhat of a radical revolutionary in his own right, but his expertise in the field of printing and publishing was second to none in China, and eventually earned him a reputation and the proud nickname "The Father of the Chinese Newspaper."

Wang Tao, like Charlie, was no ordinary Chinese. Like Sun Yat-sen and Charlie, he was a member of a very small but unique subset of Chinese in the nineteenth century whose thinking and character were profoundly influenced both by Western Christian missionaries and by time spent living in Europe or America. Their humble origins and shared experiences, forged in the fires of democracy and individualism, united them into a sort of de facto revolutionary political party that unexpectedly altered China's destiny. In the early years, they had no formal recognized authority, but by the beginning of the twentieth century they were well aware both of each other and of their unique position to radically influence China's future. It is almost inconceivable that Charlie Soong and Wang Tao did not know each other in the tightknit world of pre-revolution Shanghai, where so many of these Western trained Chinese scholars/businessmen/revolutionaries lived.

Wang Tao was significantly older than both Charlie and Sun Yat-sen, but it was reformers like him and others in his generation that made up the proverbial shoulders upon which Sun Yat-sen would stand. Born in Suzhou in 1828, Wang first worked for missionaries as a translator of the New Testament after failing the national scholar exams that would have qualified him to work in the government. The connections and experience he subsequently acquired working for and with Westerners afforded him opportunities to travel the world from Scotland to Japan and many places in between. Wang's revolutionary fervor was also forged in the raging fires of China's Taiping Rebellion after being put on the Qing Government's "most wanted" list for a scathing critique of them in a letter he wrote. Most famously, however, Wang became known as the "Father of the Chinese Newspaper" after his founding of the first Chinese daily newspaper, the *Universal Circulating Herald*, in Hong Kong in 1874.[6]

Regardless of how Charlie learned about the printing business, it was just getting off the ground when he received a letter from a Durham friend that updated him on recent happenings in and around Durham. Much to his chagrin, among the contents of the letter was news of a rumor floating around Durham that he had abandoned his Christianity and reverted to his "heathen" ways. Hurt and shocked, Charlie took the opportunity to write one more letter to the *Raleigh Christian Advocate*. The letter, headed with the simple title "A Letter From Charley Soon," begins by vociferously denying the rumor that he had abandoned Christianity and was now once again "worshipping idols" the way he had before his conversion.

Dear Bro. Reid: Will you kindly permit me a space in your valuable columns to say a few words by way of correcting a false rumor which has been circulated in some quarters of North Carolina concerning me? I am informed by a letter from a friend that it was reported in his city that I "had gone back to the heathen custom of worshipping idols." I write this to say that there *is not a particle of truth in it*. The idea of giving up my precious Savior Jesus, and returning to the worship of the lifeless gods of wood and stone, had never entered my head at any time ever since I was converted. It would be a foolish thing for a man to give up the eternal life for everlasting death.

But the originator of the false rumor may say Solomon was the wisest man that ever lived, and yet he afterwards worshipped idols. Why not any one else do the same? My answer to this is, I am not so wise as Solomon was, nor am I so foolish as he has been. But the writer does claim to have sense enough to serve his Lord to the best of his ability. And he will continue to do so as long as he liveth.

My reason for leaving the Mission was it did not give me sufficient to live upon. I could not support myself, wife and children, with about fifteen dollars of United States money per month. I hope that my friends will understand that my leaving the Mission does not mean the giving up of preaching Christ and him crucified.

At present, I am connected with the American Bible Society, but I am still doing mission work connected with our Church. My co-laborers in the Lord, Brothers Hill and Bonnell, will bear testimony to this. So my leaving the Mission simply means that I am an independent worker of our Methodist Mission, or one who tries to do as much as he can for the Mission without depending on the Church at home for his support.

I am now in charge of our new Methodist Church, which is the gift of Brother Moore, of Kansas City (U.S.A), and which is the finest native church in the China.

We have a very large Sunday school in this Church and a fine staff of teachers. I myself also have a nice Sunday School class which is composed of young men and old. We enjoy the "International Sunday-school sessions" very much. Should any of you chance to call on some Sunday morning, we will give a never-to-be-forgotten welcome, and show you how well the children can say their lessons.

I hope that those who have heard that I "had gone back to the heathen custom of worshipping idols," will kindly take the trouble to read these few lines and see for themselves wherein I stand. I am enjoying my religion and hope all my friends do theirs.

Finally, friends, I have a request to ask of you, that is, first, pray for me that I may be a useful instrument in winning souls to Christ. Second, pray for the Mission work in this benighted land, and third, pray to the Lord that He may send more laborers into the field for it is white unto harvest!"

Shanghai, China, Sept. 8th, 1892[7]

When Charlie wrote this letter to his "Durham friends," it was likely several years since he had entertained any notion of ever returning to America. Indeed, even though it is obvious that Charlie still thought highly of his friends in North Carolina and still cared deeply about his reputation amongst them, his commitment to China and to a new career was now beginning to take root. Part of his newfound identity consisted of tinkering once again with the spelling of his last name by changing it from "Soon" to "Soong," a name that was destined to become a cornerstone of modern Chinese history. Coincidentally, Charlie and his wife would also decide to begin their family around this time. Most importantly, it was sometime around this time that Charlie would begin thinking more seriously about ways in which he could more profoundly change and influence the world around him. His work as a missionary may have been rooted in good intentions, but it wasn't paying the bills (especially when the lowly status of a native preacher was permanently bestowed upon him), and China seemed to be faced with larger, more pressing problems than mission work was capable of addressing. The many duties and responsibilities that Charlie began taking on in the 1890s, many of them seemingly contradictory, begin to collide in Charlie's life almost as soon as his first child was born.

Like all newly minted graduates, Sun Yat-sen was full of hope and enthusiasm upon his graduation from the Hong Kong College of Medicine for the Chinese in 1892. If ever there were a time when Sun thought of settling down and living a conventional life within the traditional bounds of society, it would have been now. Only twenty-five years old, Sun had come a long way from his peasant roots. Now his newly acquired university education and medical degree would theoretically open even more doors of opportunity for him and allow him to take the world by storm. Indeed, right up through his graduation, it was perhaps plausible that he was not so different from the millions of college students in the world who had come before him. Certainly it was possible, his parents likely hoped anyway, that Sun was just another college student going through a rebellious phase during his adolescent and college years. Only the passage of time would tell.

It is perhaps more the province of philosophy than history to speculate the extent to which seemingly trivial and insignificant events are capable of shaping the world. It is arguable, however, that the disappointment that Sun Yat-sen faced in the months and years after his graduation was influential in shaping not only the rest of his life, but the rest of Chinese history. Sun may have been ready to embrace the world after his graduation, but the world was not nearly so enthusiastic about returning his embrace. His outlook and persona may have undergone radical changes since his childhood in the tiny rural town of Cuiheng, but China itself was still not so ready to transform. As Sun himself soon discovered, the same problem that plagued medical missionaries in China for decades—the refusal of the Chinese to view Western medicine with any modicum of respect—would radically impact his career potential after graduation. As far as most Chinese were concerned at the time, from peasants on up, his degree in Western medicine was only as valuable as the paper it was written on.[8]

Outside of landing a job at a mission hospital somewhere in China, an occupation that certainly didn't garner much respect from Chinese of any social class, Sun's career prospects were dimmer with every day that passed after graduation. His interest in politics, on the other hand, never faded. In fact, it only increased as he became aware of a unique phenomenon in China in the late nineteenth century that offered him one last chance at salvaging a "respectable" career. Overseas Chinese (the term for Chinese who live in a country outside China) like Sun Yat-sen and Charlie Soong were not at all unique in China in the late 1800s. Coastal Chinese had been spilling over the borders of southern China for decades before 1900, and they were returning to China with valuable skills and knowledge from abroad that potentially offered much to the cause of China's progress. And although they had little chance of becoming legitimate government officials on account of the strict traditions governing membership in China's elite upper echelon of government, some of them were able to find work with the mandarins because a large number of high level officials in the Qing government "were in the habit of engaging a number of advisers, working without official titles, to help them in their political and administrative tasks." In other words, Qing government officials occasionally hired men like Sun (and Charlie Soong) who had knowledge and experience that they lacked, especially knowledge of foreign ideas, cultures, and languages, even if the men they hired did not have formal, traditional educations or sprang from peasant backgrounds.

As Sun's prospects for a career in medicine dimmed, his thoughts turned increasingly toward becoming one of the self-styled pedigreed mutts in the service of Chinese officials that he had heard and read so much about in the newspapers and in conversations with his friends. He was well aware that his humble background meant that his potential was limited in the world of Chinese government and politics, but at least some chance existed; perhaps at long last he would have the opportunity to transform his words into actions regarding all of his talk about reforming China. It was a risky bet that he would ever be accepted at all into the world of Qing Dynasty government ministers and court officials that he'd heard so much about, but it was a risk worth taking.

Sun's efforts to work his way into a position of influence in the Qing government culminated in a trip to the northern Chinese city of Tianjin, just outside Beijing, in 1894. His main goal was to petition the high-ranking Qing government official, Li Hongzhang (李鴻章), but historians since then have speculated about additional possible motives. Some say the trip had a covert revolutionary aim. Others have pegged it as a possible publicity stunt, while yet other writers have speculated that Sun was essentially attempting to orchestrate an impromptu job interview. A key passage from the petition, for example, sounds more like a resume than a political reform document. "I have passed English medical examinations in Hong Kong…In my youth I experienced overseas studies. The languages of the West, its literature, its political science, its customs, its mathematics, its geography, its physics and chemistry—all these I have had the chance to study."[9]

Regardless of its real purpose, the petition trip to Tianjin was a failure. Li refused to even acknowledge Sun, much less hear out his petition. Sun persisted, however, and managed to find at least one outlet for his petition by way of a Shanghai missionary magazine known in English as the *Globe Magazine,* a periodical edited by none other than Charlie Soong's missionary supervisor, Dr. Allen, the man who would be one of the first traceable links between Charlie and Sun Yat-sen. It would be Sun's first taste of mass media publicity, but not his last.

Sometime following his rejection by Li Hongzhang and the publication of his petition in the *Globe Magazine,* Sun sailed back to Hawaii. It is not known whether his trip to Hawaii at this time was for the specific purpose of organizing a secret society, but that is what happened. Western missionaries first discovered so-called "secret societies" in China back in the nineteenth century, and since then their mysterious origins and opaque existence have intrigued and fascinated outsiders with names like the Triads and the Red Gang. Secret societies in China have such a long history that entire tomes have been written about them, despite the fact that their covert nature makes them difficult subjects to research. Secret societies were typically organized in Chinese history around religious, political, and social dissent, and different parts of China seemed to breed different types of these secret societies with different aims (political change, religious freedom, social change). Regardless, they all drew their members largely from the peasant class and from other poor, marginalized, and displaced elements of society, both of which China has never lacked, and which were found in particular abundance in nineteenth century China.[10]

In addition to providing a voice and outlet to the disenfranchised masses of China who otherwise were largely ignored by the tiny fraction of China's population that made up the ruling elite, secret societies also provided a sort of underground legal and judicial system for lower class Chinese, who were often deprived of access to a reliable police force and a formal judicial and legal system. Accordingly, such secret society groups often offered intensely practical benefits to those who joined them, so much so that failing to join a secret society could easily mean jeopardizing one's social and economic status. This was especially true of displaced and itinerant Chinese, who benefited tremendously from the aid and assistance provided by secret societies when they found themselves in a new city or country. These secret societies were the networking tools of the nineteenth century common man in China; they were also the social groups that provided essential services and relationships to the many outcasts and misfits of Chinese society that had no alternative support system.

As Chinese society quite literally began unraveling during the nineteenth century, such outcasts, misfits, rebels, and rootless wanderers almost became the rule rather than the exception in China. Decade after decade of civil war, foreign invasions, and mass insurrection translated into millions upon millions of homeless itinerants, discarded soldiers, and uprooted peasants. Throwing fuel on the fire was the ever expanding influence of Western missionaries and business men preaching Western values of democracy, equality, and individualism, exponentially increasing the discontent and dissatisfaction of millions upon millions of frustrated Chinese ever more eager to pursue their own goals and dreams rather than passively accepting their fate as had countless generations before them in China.

Of all Chinese secret societies, the Triads are among the most famous. Initially organized after the fall of the Ming Dynasty in 1644, their stated main goal was one of *fan qing fu ming*, aka "overthrowing the Qing government and restoring the Ming."

As the centuries progressed, Triad groups remained intact, but often strayed from or expanded on their original purpose. Many became involved in other more brazenly criminal pursuits ranging from smuggling, extortion, and protection rackets. Despite this, by the late nineteenth century, the possibility of actually overthrowing the Qing was again becoming a realistic aim of the Triads. By the turn of the twentieth century, other secret societies were also ubiquitous in China and could range anywhere from legitimate organizations focused purely on social or political reform, to mutual aid societies, to downright purely criminal enterprises, and everything in between.

Sun Yat-sen was certainly closely affiliated with secret societies and many other groups and organizations throughout his life. It wasn't until 1894 at the age of twenty-eight, however, that he would organize one of his own. Ironically enough, its formation would take place not in China, but on the island of Hawaii, as Sun knew he would have enough support amongst overseas Chinese there to formally organize it. The timing couldn't have been better, after all. The Beiyang Fleet (北洋艦隊), the pride and joy of the supposedly rejuvenated Chinese military, had just recently suffered its disastrous defeat off the coast of Korea at the hands of Japan. Morale was at an all-time low in China, and confidence in the leadership of the Qing regime in Beijing was waning by the day. The fruits of revolution were clearly ripening, and Sun Yat-sen was as aware of the fact as anyone in China.

The Xing Zhong Hui (興中會), also known as the Revive China Society, was formally established in a small, wooden two-level home in Honolulu on a quiet November night in 1894. Approximately twenty overseas Chinese merchants and tradesman attended the meeting, some of them baptized Christians and many, if not all, with roots in and around Canton. In an interesting Western twist on the initiation ceremonies practiced by Chinese secret societies, the oath that every man in the room took consisted of placing their right hand on a bible and swearing allegiance to the principles of the Xing Zhong Hui. The principals and purpose of the organization did not specifically mention overthrowing the Qing dynasty or establishing a republican government; perhaps they considered such explicitness unnecessary. It merely invited members to "give new life" to China through their participation and activities in the organization. It may not have been a grand affair with elaborate rituals and absolute authority, but it was a start. The humble little meeting would have repercussions for generations to come.[11]

Three months later in Hong Kong, a second branch of the Xing Zhong Hui would be organized. It would not only be larger, but it would also be more influential because it would merge with an already existent political activist group known rather grandiosely as the *Fu Ren Wen She* (復仁文社), the Literary Society for the Development of Benevolence. It would be this group that in the coming months would organize their first official rebellion aimed at destabilizing the Qing regime, the Canton Uprising of 1895.

CHAPTER 10

A REVOLUTIONARY IS BORN

·᭬᭬·

SOMETIME IN BETWEEN PRINTING BIBLES and selling them in the early 1890s, Charlie Soong became convinced of the need for radical change in China, and that the overthrow of the emperor of China was the only possible means to that end. Consequently, his participation quietly began in the revolution that would eventually bring down the governmental model of dynastic rule that had existed in China for over two thousand years. From the moment he made up his mind, he would never turn back.

Meeting Sun Yat-sen for the first time may not have been the original spark that ignited Charlie's interest in revolution, but it would have a profound impact on both his future and the future of China. There are no historically verifiable accounts of the fateful first meeting between Charlie and Sun, but it is safe to assume that the two men got along well from the moment of their introduction in 1894. Both men had spent many years living overseas where their minds became saturated with Western principles and ideals. At the same time, both developed a keen critical eye toward China and its inability to adapt to the modern world. On top of it all, both men were baptized Christians, though perhaps with different motivations and experiences in regards to their Christianity.

As Charlie made his own leap into the turbulent and dangerous waters of revolutionary China in partnership with Sun Yat-sen, he did so as surreptitiously as possible. He was, after all, growing wealthier every day, and his family was growing larger every year. After the success of his Bible printing operation, he soon expanded into printing English language books. He also began quietly printing revolutionary pamphlets and booklets during off hours at his print shop, thus allowing him to maintain a low profile in regards to his revolutionary fervor and support. In the meantime, he would make every attempt to live out a normal a life as possible, both because that is the way he wanted it and because living such a life would offer potential protection against him being suspected of illicit activity. It was at this time that Charlie's "normal" life consisted of working in his printing business, going to church, volunteering for Sunday school teaching duties, and most importantly of all, becoming a father.

Charlie's first child was born in 1890. Two more girls and three boys were to follow in the ensuing years. In order of birth their names were Ai-ling, Ching-ling, Tse-Ven (T. V.), May-ling, Tse Liang (T. L.), and Tse An (T. A.). In later years, long after Charlie's death, his children would fondly recall their childhood with a sense of nostalgia. What seemed to set Charlie apart most from his Shanghai contemporaries was his unorthodox nature and independence of thought, especially in regards to Chinese culture. Charlie's seven years in America had been far more influential in the shaping of his character and personality than he ever could have predicted. "He was very frank and outspoken," wrote one biographer, and his forthright manner of speaking was one of the obvious manifestations of his American influence.[1] Partially as a result of it, he was candid and outspoken in a way that few of his fellow Chinese were.

The first large house Charlie built in Hongkew was, not surprisingly, "half-Chinese" and "half-foreign." His decision to build the house "out in the wilderness," far from the city center, was yet another reason for his friends to consider him eccentric, as was his hobby of gardening in his vegetable garden (no respectable or educated Chinese of the time would think of farming as a hobby). Inside the house was furniture both foreign and Chinese; bedrooms were equipped with distinctly American-style mattresses, a luxury that "neighbors would come in just to peer at." Charlie's preference for Western food (especially from the American South), rather than Chinese, was the proverbial icing on the cake of his odd and unorthodox character in the eyes of his Chinese friends. After some time, even Mrs. Soong gave up trying to convert Charlie back to his culinary Chinese roots and became an "excellent foreign-style cook."

By all accounts, Charlie's everyday life in Shanghai was enjoyable, but it was anything but ordinary. Its unpredictable nature would take on a new meaning with his decision to begin lending support to Sun Yat-sen and the revolutionaries in Shanghai. If he ever had hopes for the safety and security that most people strive to realize in life, he surely and knowingly sacrificed them in the name of a cause he thought higher and more valuable. Of almost everyone involved in the revolutionary activities organized by men such as Sun Yat-sen, few had more to lose than Charlie Soong.

Historians have called Charlie Soong many things. He has been dubbed a Christian missionary, an entrepreneur, and a revolutionary. All of these are true, but other critical components of Charlie's character and historical significance have been largely overlooked. One of these regards the severe, irrefutable, albeit deliberate danger he immersed himself in on the day he decided to support Sun Yat-sen and his plans for a revolution. Charlie's decision to begin secretly printing revolutionary materials on his company printing presses in Shanghai, and later his decision to act as the de facto treasurer of the revolution, were certainly not made without full knowledge of all potential risks. Charlie was keenly aware of the fate that befell Lu Haodong (陸皓東), Sun Yat-sen's childhood friend, after the Canton Uprising in 1895. The Qing government, like all dynasties before them, did not take kindly to revolutionaries, and traditional Chinese forms of justice were still in play well into the twentieth century in China. This meant that Charlie not only put himself in extreme danger by participating in the revolution, he also put his family in the same danger. Traditional Chinese values were rooted heavily in the concept of family solidarity, and this meant that just as the actions of an individual could rain down honor upon both him and his entire family, dishonorable actions could also bring down punishment upon not only him, but also his entire family. Sun Yat-sen's family was well aware of this when they quickly picked up and moved from their hometown in China to distant Hawaii in the wake of the failed 1895 Canton Uprising, which had put Sun on the Chinese government's most wanted list.

The danger that Charlie voluntarily put himself and his family in by not only associating with revolutionary activists in Shanghai but by actively participating in the publishing and printing of anti-Manchu, pro-revolutionary materials are historically important for two reasons. One, Charlie's participation in revolutionary activities necessitated his keeping an extremely low profile in regards to any activities related to the revolution. Nothing made more sense and nothing was more effective at protecting him and his family from harm than staying as anonymous as possible in regards to his revolutionary activities and sentiments. Two, and most unfortunate for historians, Charlie became very skilled at the art of covering his tracks. As a result, there is little today in the way of stories or documents that chronicle Charlie's activities during this crucial phase of the revolution's beginning because Charlie was so careful in this regard. His life and his family's depended on his utmost discretion.

Despite the chaos that unfolded in much of China in the decade before and after the turn of the twentieth century, Charlie Soong, and many successful businessmen like him in and around Shanghai, grew more successful by the year. Charlie's printing business and his extremely lucrative work as a *comprador*, a term popular in China at the time that designated a manager whose main responsibility was negotiating deals and contracts between Chinese and Western companies, for the Fou Foong Flour Mill, gradually elevated him into the upper class of Shanghai society by the turn of the century. While it is true that Charlie's business success in Shanghai led to wealth he never dreamed of as a youth, wealthy merchants and entrepreneurs were a dime a dozen in early twentieth century Shanghai. What would truly end up separating Charlie from the rest of the Shanghai elite and really help launch his name into the annals of Chinese history would be his children, and an unusual but fateful decision Charlie would make in regards to their education.

Much has been written about Charlie's decision to send his children overseas for their educations while they were still so young. He has often been hailed by historians as being a great fan of American education and one of the first Chinese proponents of female education because of his decision to send his daughters to the United States for their schooling. His progressive thinking was not without cost though, as many of his friends and associates in Shanghai thought him to be just shy of insane for spending so much money to not only educate his daughters, but to educate them overseas.

Educating daughters was something not considered by most Chinese, even in the more progressive areas of China around the turn of the twentieth century, and higher education of women was still something in its infancy even in the United States. Charlie's friends and associates may have thought him foolish for spending so much money on the education of his daughters, but it did not dissuade him. His determination to educate *all* of his children, not just the boys, remained steadfast throughout his life, as did his reputation for being unorthodox and unconventional even in what was then arguably considered to be the most progressive and cosmopolitan city in Asia.

While Charlie may have certainly been a proponent of women's education, it does not seem that sending his children abroad at such a young age was an event he relished. What was likely a larger factor looming over the head of Charlie Soong in regards to his decision to have his children educated abroad was the tremendous danger they faced by staying in China. The execution of criminals was a practice with a long history in China, but the execution of (or other serious retribution) the families of criminals was also not unusual. Charlie Soong knew as well as any other Chinese of his time the ruthless brutality and revenge-inspired justice that the Chinese legal system was capable of meting out. Unlike, Sun Yat-sen, whose family members were usually safely abroad in Hawaii or Japan, Charlie and his family slept and resided in Shanghai, where things always had the potential of turning bad very quickly. While Sun was almost always abroad, Charlie, his wife, and his family breathed danger in Shanghai every day of every week. The danger may have ebbed and flowed over the years, but it was ever present. Indeed, it is clear that

Charlie Soong was not only willing to sacrifice his own life for the sake of revolution in China, he was also willing to sacrifice the futures, and perhaps even the very lives, of those he loved most.

⸙

It was Charlie who is said to have supplied Sun with his first "donation" in the form of a three thousand yuan contribution for the express purpose of founding the Xing Zhong Hui in 1895.[2] More importantly, it was Charlie Soong in Shanghai who wrote a letter to Sun Yat-sen in Hawaii soon afterwards advising him to return to China as soon as possible in the tumultuous wake of the Sino-Japanese War. The purpose of the letter was to inform Sun that discontent was running high in China and the time was perfect for an uprising. Sun wasted no time getting back to Hong Kong in order to establish a local branch of the Xing Zhong Hui in February of 1895. The establishment of the Hong Kong Xing Zhong Hui significantly expanded its size and they set immediately about planning the uprising that they hoped would be the beginning of the end for the Qing Dynasty.

As the summer months passed, Sun continued to make plans and to recruit new Xing Zhong Hui members both in Hong Kong and in Canton, where his real connections lay in the form of family relations and old childhood friends who were now scattered throughout the region. One reason that Canton was in fact chosen as the sight of the planned uprising was Sun's influence in the region. Although not a major player by any means in China at this point, Sun's Canton base of support would serve him extremely well in the coming decades.

By autumn of 1895, the stage and date was finally and officially set for the long-planned uprising. It was to commence in

Hong Kong on October 26 with a boatload of weapons and Sun's loyal (and sometimes paid) followers bound for nearby Canton. Upon arrival, they were to be quietly greeted by a throng of fellow Xing Zhong Hui members at the port, and from there were to begin their attacks on government buildings and officials. As an omen of future rebellions planned by Sun, however, his plan did not unfold; it unraveled. The uprising quickly devolved into a debacle of epic proportions with fatal consequences for some involved.

On October 26, 1895, Sun and his men were prepared for the arrival of the Hong Kong boat when Sun received a telegram telling him that the ship would be delayed twenty-four hours. In response, Sun canceled the entire operation and sent a telegram back to Hong Kong saying as much. The telegram failed to arrive on time, however, and the boat full of weapons and men departed Hong Kong as originally planned. When it arrived in Canton, it was met not by Sun and his supporters but by garrisons of government troops, who had been tipped off by some government officials in Hong Kong. The local magistrate was lenient on most of the rebels, but a small number were chosen as probable leaders and sent to the execution block. One of them was Sun's childhood friend and loyal follower, Lu Hao Dong, a man still considered a national hero in China today.

Some revolutions, despite the oceans of blood spilled and the multitudes of lives lost, have an air of drama, romance, and righteousness to them. They gradually and dramatically unfold in story-like sequence with heroes, villains, and a sense of inevitable destiny. The American Revolution and the French Revolution are often viewed in this light. The uprisings and conflicts in China that eventually brought down the last emperor of China tended to be significantly more spasmodic and anticlimactic, however.

One reason is that the Chinese Revolution did not involve two well-organized opposition groups. The Chinese Imperial Army was an official government entity, but the revolutionaries that opposed it lacked not only training, but any semblance of formal and centralized authority. Sun Yat-sen may have envisioned himself at this point in history as the leader of a movement whose purpose it was to overthrow the Qing Empire, but the reality remained that he had no experience in either military or political matters, and that the few hundred men following him consisted mostly of discontents and pseudo-gang members who were by no means representative of the Chinese population at large. Furthermore, his pro-revolutionary activities were so small and so localized that to the few that had ever even heard of him viewed him as little more than a harmless local rabble-rouser.

Sun Yat-sen managed to safely escape Canton despite the fact that his name was somehow leaked out as being the leader of the uprising. From this moment onwards, however, he would be branded an outlaw and be included on every "most wanted" list in China for well over the next decade. Indeed, for the next sixteen years Sun would live a life of semi-permanent exile from China that would essentially transform him into a relentless peripatetic promoter of Chinese revolution. It would be soon after this that Charlie Soong's presence in Shanghai would become so crucial to the future success of Sun.

Over the course of the next decade, Charlie Soong's home in Shanghai, as well as his printing factory, would become a secret refuge for Sun Yat-sen on his frequent covert return trips to China. Although it would later become well-known that Sun stayed in the Soong house "whenever he came to Shanghai," and that Charlie's children eventually came to look upon Sun "as an uncle" and take him "as much for granted as they did any member of the family," no one at the time knew how crucial Charlie's generosity during this time would be to the future success of the revolutionary movement in China.[3]

After his escape to Hong Kong, Sun again made his way to Hawaii with the discreet help of his old Scottish missionary friend and teacher, Dr. Cantlie. Cantlie claims to have only discovered Sun's whereabouts early the following year on a return trip to England via Hawaii (Cantlie's health issues caused him to move back to England at this time) when he quite unintentionally bumped into what he thought was a Japanese national.

> The vehicle in which I was driving with my wife, and a Japanese nurse in charge of my son, through the streets of Honolulu was stopped by a Japanese looking very trim in European dress and with a mustache of respectable dimensions, who proffered his hand, raised his hat, and smiled affably. We all regarded him with astonishment; the Japanese nurse addressed him in Japanese, but he shook his head in response, and it was some time before we recognized it was Sun minus his cue and Chinese dress. A cordial greeting ensued and a visit to us in London was arranged.[4]

Sun, as it turns out, was in Hawaii after first escaping to Japan. While in Japan, news of his "revolution" in Canton made its way to the Japanese newspapers. He also apparently took ample time and expended much effort in Japan to effect an "image makeover" to help him maintain his newly minted renegade lifestyle. Fortunately for Sun, it was thoroughly and convincingly effective. After leaving Japan, Sun looked more like a svelte Japanese intellectual than any radical Chinese revolutionary renegade. By time he ran into Dr. Cantlie in Hawaii, he was virtually unrecognizable.

Cantlie's invitation to Sun to visit London did not fall on deaf ears. After traveling across the continental United States the following summer, a journey that reportedly occasionally involved surveillance by undercover Chinese imperial agents, Sun landed in London in October 1896. Although exact details regarding what happened next have been the subject of infinite speculation and debate ever since, there is no arguing its startling historical significance.

At some point after Sun's arrival in London and his warm reception by Dr. Cantlie and his family, he decided to take a walk. Just why he decided to walk by the Chinese embassy in London (a short distance from Dr. Cantlie's house) when he knew that the Chinese government had a well-publicized price on his head is anybody's guess. While it is possible that he failed to see any danger in such brazen behavior, it is not likely. Did he know precisely what he was doing and the consequences that would follow? Was he really "tricked" as he claimed he was in his later writings? Perhaps no one will never know. What is known is that after engaging in some small talk with Chinese guards at the embassy, he was suddenly grabbed, whisked inside, and held captive for the next several days. Not surprisingly, Cantlie and others had no idea where Dr. Sun had gone in the days after his abduction. His disappearance remained a mystery, according to Dr. Cantlie, until he received a knock at his door late one night. Upon opening the door, he discovered no one there. There was, however, a handwritten note providing Cantlie with his first clue regarding Sun's whereabouts.

There is a friend of yours imprisoned in the Chinese
Legation here since last Sunday; they intend sending him

out to China, where it is certain they will hang him. It is very sad for the poor man, and unless something is done at once he will be taken away and no one will know it. I dare not sign my name, but this is the truth, so believe what I say. His name is, I believe, Sin Yin Sen.[5]

Cantlie would later reveal the writer of this letter as the wife of a local Chinese embassy (legation) employee who overheard conversations about Sun and his fate. Cantlie sprang to action. After finding only apathy in pursuing governmental and diplomatic channels, he embarked on a mission to publicize the plight of his friend that would rival any modern-day public relations professional. Being a man of some reputation in London at the time, he was able to convince local newspapers to write articles about the plight of the "kidnapped leader of the Chinese revolution." A media frenzy ensued until finally the British government took notice and put the Chinese embassy under twenty-four hour surveillance and gave explicit orders aimed at them not to engage in any activity regarding kidnapping or illegally extraditing any person in the country—including visitors. The Chinese embassy soon relented and released Sun after nearly two weeks of captivity.

There's no denying the bizarre and borderline suicidal nature of Sun's behavior in the lead-up to this incident. Likewise, there is also no denying the monumental impact that the incident had on Sun's future. Prior to the London kidnapping, no one outside of China had heard of the man named Sun Yat-sen. Even his reputation inside China teetered back and forth amongst the few who knew of his existence between that of a revolutionary reformer and that of a rabble-rousing criminal instigator. After the London kidnapping, however, and with the help of Dr. Cantlie's brilliant manipulation of the British media, Sun Yat-sen now had a new title: "Leader of the Chinese Revolution." Not only that, but his fame and reputation would spread worldwide. If Sun had planned for things to turn out the way they did, he was proving to be a genius beyond anyone's dreams.

⤬

Charlie naturally took precautions took protect himself from possible retaliation for his participation in revolutionary activities, but he eventually discovered that one of the best ways of mitigating the risk for his children was to send them to America. And send them he did. His oldest child, Ai-ling, was the first to go. In 1904 Ai-ling was only fourteen years old, but after spending several years at the McTyeire School for Girls (and boarding there while school was in session since the age of seven), a recently opened Methodist-sponsored school in Shanghai, she was registered at Wesleyan College in Macon, Georgia. Her enrollment at Wesleyan was not random. Charlie would have perhaps chosen Vanderbilt or Trinity College (which had relocated to Durham, North Carolina, in the early 1890s, a few decades before it changed its name to Duke University), but like almost every other institution of higher learning in the world at the time, they still maintained all-male enrollment policies. Wesleyan College was suggested as a possibility by Charlie's Vanderbilt classmate and friend Bill Burke, who hailed from Macon. Burke not only helped Ai-ling gain admission to Wesleyan through hometown connections, but he offered to accompany her on the long journey there in 1904.

The trip to America was not nearly as smooth as the travelers had hoped it would be. After departing from Shanghai, the ship soon stopped over in Japan. While there, Burke's wife became gravely ill. He had no choice but to stay behind while Ai-ling continued her journey with the aid of only a few recent acquaintances. Upon her arrival in San Francisco, customs officials, who did their best to enforce the anti-Chinese immigration policies put in place over two decades before by the U.S. government, detained Ai-ling and threatened to have her permanently confined, partly on account of a "back door" Portuguese passport that Charlie insist she carry in case she encountered trouble as a Chinese national getting into the United States. After several days, she was finally released.[6]

The rest of Ai-ling's journey to Macon was without incident, but that didn't mean there wasn't some fanfare along the way. A few weeks before her 1904 arrival, an article appeared in the *Durham Sun* anticipating her visit to Durham under the caption "Will Visit This City; Facts Regarding Rev. Chas J. Soon and his daughter, Miss Alice."

> Several years ago, Trinity Methodist Sunday School took charge of the education of Charlie Soon, who was brought and introduced into the school by Rev. T. Page Ricaud, of Wilmington. The school and friends educated Charlie, and provided for all his wants for several years. They sent him to Trinity and Vanderbilt, and he returned to China, and was there a source of great usefulness to the church and to our missionaries, who were laboring there in behalf of Christianity. Dr. Rhade, who visited here coming from China some two years ago, having been a missionary in China for some thirty years, spoke most highly of Charlie and the valuable services he had rendered them.

Friends in the city have heard this week from Charlie
and he is sending his daughter, Alice, his oldest child, to
the Southern Wesleyan Female College at Macon, GA,
to be thoroughly educated, and when she has received
the benefit of an education at Wesleyan, and then she
takes a course of medicine, and is to be made an M.D,
and then she returns to China, to act as medical missionary among the Chinese woman and children. She is
a very bright girl, and will stay in this country until she
is thoroughly educated, and prepared for the degree of
M.D. and will return to China. Charlie Soon has accu-
mulated considerable wealth but he is still a great friend
to religion, and interests himself largely in promoting
the cause of Christianity. He is now Private Secretary
to the nephew of Li Hung Chang, the most prominent
man perhaps in China. Charlie is very well thought of
indeed, stands very high, and is a man of great usefulness
and ability. It is more than likely that his daughter, Miss
Alice, will spend next Summer, or a portion of it, visiting
friends in Durham. Charlie remembers his friends here
very kindly, and sends his best love to all his friends, and
to Trinity Church and Trinity Sunday School.[7]

As the article reveals, it was Ai-ling's original intention to
enroll in medical school, perhaps with the intent of becoming a
medical missionary just as Charlie hoped to do twenty years earlier. It is also curious to note that Charlie is mentioned as being
secretary to the nephew of Li Hung Chang, the most powerful
statesman in the Qing government at the time. While the statement suggests a possible previously unknown, not to mention
unlikely, association between the two men, it is just as likely that

the claim was erroneous or simply the result of someone's over-active imagination.

Despite her relatively smooth transition to American college life, Ai-ling never forgot the painful memories of her confinement in San Francisco, and she did not hesitate to bring it up in conversation with Americans in the future. For years afterwards, she took the opportunity to relate the story of her confinement to anyone willing to listen, including U.S. President Theodore Roosevelt. Just how Ai-ling Soong came to be able to tell the painful story of her confinement to President Roosevelt was a story as entertaining as it was curious in the lore of the Soong family.

A mere twenty years before Ai-ling's visit to Washington, D. C., her father was a penniless student in America with little in the way of future prospects. In a matter of two decades, he managed to rise to rise to such prominence and forge such high-level social bonds that his own daughter one day found herself in a face-to-face conversation with the president of the United States. The visit came about as a result of Charlie's relationship with his old friend B. C. Wen, who was now also his brother-in-law (Charlie's wife and Wen's wife were sisters). Much like Charlie, Wen's fascinating career would also take many twists and turns in the years after his return to China from America in 1881 as a student in the Chinese Educational Mission. After returning to China, Wen spent several years working in various U.S. consulates in China. In 1905, however, he was appointed secretary and advisor to Viceroy Duan Fang (端方), one of the top-ranking officials of the Qing government. Soon after his appointment, a tour was organized that took several senior-ranking Qing government officials to the United States and Europe (五大臣出洋) in order to study their respective constitutional governments, and

Wen accompanied them.[8] It was during his visit to Washington, D. C. that he and Charlie made arrangements for Ai-ling to come up from Georgia for a visit.

"America is very beautiful, and I am very happy here, but why do you call it a free country?" she unapologetically asked President Roosevelt with all the stark directness of her father. "Why should a Chinese girl be kept out of the country if it is so free? We would never treat visitors to China like that. America is supposed to be the land of liberty."[9]

The visit of Ai-ling and her uncle to the White House illustrated the remarkably complicated nature of early twentieth century politics and society in China. B. C. Wen was a respected Qing government official, and Charlie, at least on the surface, was nothing more than a successful Shanghai businessman and active church member. Behind the scenes, however, Charlie was an underground revolutionary helping to plot the overthrow of the very government in which Wen was employed. It is even reasonable to imagine that Charlie's activities and relationship with Sun Yat-sen had the full blessing and tacit approval of Wen, who was certainly one of the more progressive-minded individuals in the service of the Qing government. But this was the nature of society in pre-revolution China. Personal relationships, political activities, religious affiliations, and almost every other relationship in Chinese society were part of an immense, complicated, and often contradictory web of existence that Chinese of the day simply got used to navigating on a daily basis. This is not to say, however, that the complicated web of contradictory relationships never involved a price to be paid, as both Wen and Soong would eventually realize.

Ai Ling's sisters and brothers would soon follow in her footsteps to the United States with their education as the ostensible reason for their departure, but their safety was likely an equal-ly important motivation. After attending local mission-spon-sored schools in Shanghai, Ching-ling would follow Ai-ling to Wesleyan, as would Mei-ling. Mei-ling, however, would break the family record as far as age of enrollment was concerned. At the mere age of ten, partially because of her own stubborn insis-tence, she would accompany Ching-ling to the United States to pursue her education first in New Jersey, then at Wesleyan. She was, of course, too young to enroll at Wesleyan when she arrived and alternative arrangements had to be made for her in order to fulfill her studies. Numerous publications have chronicled the experiences of the Soong brothers and sisters in America, partic-ularly those of the three Soong daughters. In later decades the stories of their experiences would provide Americans with a new perspective on China and the Chinese at a time when it was criti-cally needed, particularly in the decades before World War II.

It wasn't until 1905 that Charlie himself would make his first trip back to the United States since leaving in 1885. Although often mistakenly alleged, the purpose of his trip was not to ac-company Ai-ling to school in Georgia (she began her studies at Wesleyan the year before), but rather to pursue an agenda of a far less personal, and far more revolutionary, nature. It was in 1905 that Sun Yat-sen would organize the largest and most influential of his "secret" societies. Known as the Tongmenghui (同盟會), or the Revolutionary Alliance, it was destined to be the organization that would be the unifying force behind the even-tual success of the revolutionary movement in China. And it was Charlie Soong who was chosen to be not only its treasurer, but also one of its chief fund-raisers.

While in the process of organizing the Revolutionary Alliance, it was quickly realized that the revolution had little

chance of succeeding without a constant supply of funds to finance it. To that end, a fund-raising scheme was concocted by
Sun Yat-sen and his fellow revolutionaries in Japan, whereby the
Revolutionary Alliance was to raise funds by issuing a series of
bonds that were to be sold to all "interested parties" around
the world. In exchange for their financial support, bond buyers
would be rewarded with special status in the newly established
Republic of China—the sovereign entity that was to be created
by a successful revolution. To this end, Sun Yat-sen had bonds
printed in Japan that were to serve as "IOU's for very high interest loans."[10] He'd had such bonds printed before for the purpose of selling to overseas Chinese around the world in order to
raise money for the revolution, but now his efforts, as well as the
cost of the bonds, were redoubled. Soon after the founding of
the Revolutionary Alliance, Sun left for Indochina, where from
October 1905 to February 1906 he "tried to sell patriotic bonds
to the wealthy Chinese traitors in the local community."[11] At the
same time Sun left for Indochina and Europe, Charlie Soong
embarked on his American tour.

Charlie's attendance at the organizational meeting of the
Revolutionary Alliance in Japan is difficult to verify owing to his
penchant for secretiveness, but it's almost certain that he attended the meetings before his departure for San Francisco since
nearly every ship that sailed from Shanghai to San Francisco in
those days stopped in Japan on the way. It is also known that Sun
Yat-sen was in America the year before Charlie on a fundraising
venture. His fundraising endeavors met with little success, however, and it is only logical that, perhaps at the suggestion of Sun
himself, Charlie was now selected to try his luck with fundraising
in America. So with his wealth of knowledge about American
culture, his long list of well-connected American friends, and

a suitcase full of "patriotic bonds," Charlie Soong was sent to America in 1905 to raise funds for the revolution. And he found them.

Charlie's decision to stop first in San Francisco was a sensible and wise one. The enormous overseas Chinese population there virtually guaranteed an auspicious beginning to his nationwide fund-raising tour despite the fact that anti-Chinese sentiment was still relatively high in the United States at the time. Charlie no doubt hoped this first stop would be a fruitful one, but he had no idea how fruitful it would be. Charlie's 1905 fund-raising tour of the United States raised approximately two million dollars, and every penny of it went to the revolutionary cause.[12] He likely visited several other locations on his tour of America, but there was never much evidence that proved his visit until a newspaper article appeared in the *Raleigh News & Observer* (again, this is not a surprise given Charlie's penchant for secrecy) in 1936, over three decades after his visit. It was yet another article written in the years leading up to World War II intended to highlight North Carolina's unique relationship with China. A lucid account of Charlie's little publicized visit to Durham in the fall of 1905 is highly revealing.

> For several weeks he stayed with General Carr, as a guest at his home, Somerset, and the two men renewed their old friendship and rediscovered the strong ties of affection which bound them together. T.M. Gorman, who served for 32 years as private secretary to General Carr, says that he recalls meeting Soong at that time and had long talks with him at the old Club, which stood on the site of the present Trust Building at the corner of Main and Market Streets.

The Club, which had no other name, was the meeting place for business and professional men, and there Soong, in company with General Carr, spent long hours conversing with old college mates. Trinity College had been removed to Durham some years before, and though the years had taken their toll, their were several professors still living with whom Charlie could talk over old times in Randolph County.

Mr. Gorman, who had not known Charlie during his student days, recollects that in 1905, Soong seemed thoroughly at home in the Club, as he mingled with the businessmen of the town. He spoke excellent English, and his interests were similar to those of his old friends—business affairs, Church activities, the promising future of the college in its new setting, and the careers of his college mates.[13]

It is clear from this article that Charlie's American identity was quite well intact in 1905, as were his relationships with his old North Carolina friends. It remains unknown precisely how much fund-raising Charlie engaged in during his visit to Durham, but it would not be at all unexpected if old and powerful friends like General Carr, who was well known as a generous supporter of various political, religious, and social causes, were approached by Charlie for financial support of a Chinese revolution. Regardless, Charlie's visit to Durham reaffirmed old ties and encouraged him even more to look to America as a land of opportunity for his children.

CHAPTER 11

AN UNEXPECTED TRIUMPH

❦

T HE DECADE AFTER THE 1895 Canton Uprising in China did little to calm to fears of everyday Chinese in regards to the stability and competence of the Qing regime and even less to placate the desires and ambitions of the ever-expanding ranks of revolutionary reformers in China. After the disastrous Sino-Japanese War that stripped China of possibly every last vestige of its remaining dignity, one final attempt was made by the Qing government to initiate reform in the empire.

Although Emperor Guangxu was born into his exalted position in the 1870s, he didn't exercise his power until the 1890s, at which time his aunt, the Empress Dowager Cixi, gradually began relinquishing some power to him. Guangxu, who was then in his twenties, enthusiastically embraced the power that was coming his way by acquiring his own set of advisors to help him set policy. Not surprisingly, the advisors Guangxu chose were young, and being so were open-minded. They were so open-minded, in fact, that in the summer of 1898 Guangxu announced one of the most progressive and revolutionary reform policies in the recent history of China.

Known as the Hundred Days Reform (百日維新), the initiative honed in on educational, social, and governmental reforms aimed specifically at bringing China into the modern world. They included abolishing the traditional examination system, introducing subjects like science and civics into the Chinese curriculum in place of the study of the Chinese classics, and encouraging the development of industrialization and modern finance in the economy. For three consecutive months in the summer of 1898 the policies and programs of Guangxu and his ministers looked to be a promising spark of illumination in the damp darkness of late nineteenth century China. The reform programs that Guangxu instituted, however, contained within them the seeds of their own destruction.

Conservative Qing government officials, alarmed at the radically progressive nature of the reforms instituted by Guangxu, urged Cixi to react. She duly complied. By the end of September 1898, the Hundred Days of Reform was but a memory, and Emperor Guangxu himself was placed under house arrest. Cixi restored herself to full power, and with her restoration the last great hope for reform in China ended not with a bang, but a whimper. For the next decade, the Qing government would appear stable to outside observers, but below the surface the situation was entirely different. Weakened by decades of corruption, incompetence, and intransigence, the countdown to the end of the Qing Empire, as well as that of dynastic rule itself in China, was officially underway. By the arrival of the twentieth century, the Qing Dynasty would not need a hatchet man to bring it down. A strong wind would do the job just fine. It would take another eleven years, however, for that strong wind to blow.

It is one of modern Chinese history's greatest ironies that the man who eventually went down in history as the leader of China's 1911 Revolution was not even in China when the revolution began. Even more remarkably, the man often referred to as the "George Washington of China" did not even live in China for the fifteen years leading up to the 1911 Revolution (except for the secret return visits he made to Shanghai and the home of Charlie Soong). No one was more aware than Sun Yat-sen himself, after all, that if he did return to China, he would have been promptly arrested by Chinese authorities for his participation in the 1895 Canton Uprising.

Sun's status as one of China's most wanted rebels meant that a significant portion of his life was spent on the run, in particular the years between 1895 and 1912. During this time he lived in several different countries, including Japan, the United States, Hawaii, and Vietnam, and spent considerable amounts of time in such places trying to raise funds for a revolution and rally support among overseas Chinese communities wherever he went. It was during his secret visits back to China in the late 1890s and the first decade of the twentieth century that his relationship with Charlie and the rest of the Soong family flourished.

For more than a decade prior to the 1911 Revolution (Xinhai Revolution), there were a series of failed uprisings and rebellions in China, many of them orchestrated from afar by Sun Yat-sen or his associates. Few of the uprisings, however, were of major significance, and none posed any threat to the Qing government in Beijing. A few were so small in fact that news of their occurrence barely spread beyond local jurisdictions. As early as the spring of 1911, however, rumors were circulating again of yet another uprising in the works for October of the same year. Australian journalist William Donald, already a veteran China reporter with strong connections in many Chinese circles, described in his biography his meeting with the revolutionaries in Shanghai with equal measures of excitement and anxiety. More importantly, he provided some insight into the life and activities of Charlie Soong at this critical time.

Shanghai at the time was a hotbed of revolutionary activity partially because of its distance from the ever-watchful eye of Beijing. If the revolutionary meetings weren't conducted at Mr. Chang's park, a "cool and inviting…retreat for Chinese elite," they were, according to Donald, conducted in Charlie Soong's printing shop on Shantung Road, "where the high echelon in the underground often met." At the time, Charlie Soong's home in Shanghai, Donald confirms, "was often the intense little doctor's refuge."[1]

"Well! How's Australia's gift to confusion to the enemy!" Charlie joked upon seeing Donald in the summer of 1911, indicating a comfortable familiarity between the two men.[2] Charlie went on to tell him that "there was pressure to explode the rebellion late in October," but Donald expressed worry that after the Manchu government was toppled, no reliable and experienced government body existed to replace it. Afterwards, Donald remarked simply that Charlie "looked distressed."

The uprising planned for early October 1911 in the city of Wuchang by the Tongmenghui and a few other revolutionary groups in the city was postponed just before it was to commence due to a lack of sufficient preparation. It was perhaps an inauspicious omen, then, that the 1911 Revolution in China began anyway, largely by accident.

A sudden deafening explosion that ripped through the Russian concession in Hankou, China, on October 9, 1911, was the accidental spark of the revolution that forced the rebels to again rapidly reconsider their plans. The explosion was the result of the unintentional detonation of a bomb that was secretly being built by the local revolutionaries in a building there. In the panic-ridden minutes that ensued, the revolutionaries anxiously debated how to react, fully aware that police would soon be on their way. Local authorities quickly arrived on the scene as expected, and while investigating the explosion, they discovered the bomb factory, and inside it a roster of rebels in the area and documents that contained copies of the seal of the yet to be manifest "Republic of China." With this information they had all they needed to pursue and prosecute every rebel in the city. They tried, but were only successful in capturing a few, whom they promptly beheaded.

In the meantime the remaining rebels had to think faster than ever before. The decision at the top of their list of priorities: whether to flee from the city as soon as possible or take advantage of the confusion that the explosion caused and launch their long-planned uprising right then and there. After gathering enough momentum to reorganize, they made the fateful decision that forever altered the course of Chinese history. Storming the building of the local city government in Wuchang in the ensuing hours, the rebels forced the local magistrate to flee, appointed another local official as the leader of their movement (leaving him little choice in the matter), and duly declared themselves free of Qing rule. This fateful string of events occurred on October 10, and was subsequently dubbed Double Ten Day (雙十節). In the days and weeks following the Wuchang Uprising (sometimes referred to as the Wuhan Uprising), revolutionaries in other cities followed suit by helping to declare each free and independent of Qing rule.

An American woman who became a missionary apprentice of sorts to Charlie Soong in the years before the Wuchang Uprising described Charlie as a "small, round man with always twinkling eyes" who 'took a big-brother interest" in her and her missionary husband. In addition to often asking Charlie for advice, she would also often listen to him speak about his days in America. She recalled with particular clarity, however, her conversation with Charlie the day after the Wuchang Uprising.

The day after the Revolution was an accomplished fact in Shanghai, Mr. Soong came in beaming. "Now I can tell you all about it," he said, when he found out how excited I was about what had happened the night before. So he told me of his long friendship with Sun Yat-Sen, and how he had helped Sun in every way possible, especially with money. "Not that I ever bothered to take a receipt for the amounts I sent him," he chuckled. "Maybe you have wondered why we live so plainly here in this place?" he asked. "I haven't thought much about that," I replied, "except that I felt you and Mrs. Soong did not care for display, and I know you are very generous in your donations to church work. Also you are at a good deal of expense for the education of your children." "That is true," he said, "but I have saved all that I could to help Sun's cause, because I felt that was the best way for me to help my country." Then he chuckled again and told me how he had for some weeks been urging his sister to come down to Shanghai from the interior. He had invented a good many reasons why she should visit him at once, and he had been worried that she might not arrive in time, for of course he could not tell her that he wanted to be sure she was safe with him these date for the Revolution.[3]

The recollection of the missionary provides further testimony not only to Charlie's close relationship with Sun

Yat-sen (especially his close financial relationship), but to the extremes he went to in the name of secrecy. Charlie clearly feared for the safety of his sister who was presumably closer to the heart of the revolutionary violence in China's interior regions, yet he refused to directly tell her anything about what he knew and risk revealing his true relationship with the revolutionaries.

Sun Yat-sen later stated that he was in California when the Wuchang Uprising unexpectedly occurred, and that he did not read about it until he was on a train bound for Denver days later.[4] In subsequent days he received telegrams from Shanghai, but had trouble reading them because they were in code, and his code, he claimed, had been left in Texas. He did acknowledge finally reading them, but provided no reason for his failure to telegram any response whatsoever back to the rebel leaders in Shanghai; this left them confused as to not only his location, but his ideas on how to proceed with the revolution.

In what had become a recurring pattern in Sun's life, his response to the Wuchang Uprising was not what one might expect. His reaction to what turned out to be the spark that ignited the Chinese Revolution of 1911 was to continue his train journey to the East Coast of the United States, where he would catch the first available boat to London, and then to Paris. It has since been presumed that he was attempting to shore up diplomatic support for a new government in China because it was his belief that foreign support of a new Chinese government was more important than his immediate presence in China. Regardless, his absence from China for nearly the next three months, with no communication back to his followers in China, left the entire revolutionary movement with a leadership vacuum that severely impacted its future.[5]

Sun Yat-sen's eventual return to China on December 25, 1911, was even more of a non-event than his many covert returns to Shanghai in previous years; most of his revolutionary followers had no idea he was back. It had been nearly three months since the now famous Wuchang Uprising, and any excitement surrounding the arrival of the de-facto leader of the revolutionary movement in China had long since dissipated. Much to the surprise of the small contingent of men that met with him upon his arrival, however, Sun was not alone. Accompanying him was a most unusual figure in the history of Chinese-American relations; chronicling the whole incident was the journalist William Donald, who would go on to become one of Sun Yat-sen's closest advisors and confidants.

Homer Lea was an American born in Denver, Colorado, who met Sun in California in 1909, reportedly through Yung Wing, the first Chinese Yale graduate and the man who organized the Chinese Education Mission. Lea was attracted to Sun on account of what seemed to be his life's twin obsessions: China and the military. Though physically debilitated by a severe hunchback (said to be the result of being dropped as a baby) and many other serious maladies, the five foot three, one-hundred pound Lea fancied himself a military leader of unparalleled ability, a most capable battle savvy general destined to be the military leader who would lead the Chinese revolutionaries to their ultimate victory.

After befriending many Chinese in and around the Los Angeles Chinatown area, and studying briefly at Stanford University, Lea was so intense and single-minded in his pursuit of military greatness as a leader of the impending Chinese revolution that he once traveled to China and also became an active member of the Los Angeles area Bao Huang Hui, the Protect the

Emperor Society (an organization formed in Vancouver by high-level Chinese exiles).

Homer Lea was already in Europe for the medical treatment of one of his many maladies when Sun got the news of the Wuchang Uprising while in America, perhaps partially influencing Sun's own decision to first go to Europe instead of heading directly back to China. Lea met with Sun in London, and the two men attempted to gain at least a modicum of diplomatic recognition from both the British and French governments. Eventually, newspapers in Shanghai began to get reports of Sun's location, and of an "American general" that was supposedly traveling with him. Rumor and speculation quickly began circulating in the information vacuum created by Sun's lack of communication with anyone in China, and many wondered if Sun had somehow gotten the American military involved in China's impending revolution.

"American generals?" exclaimed one rebel leader in Shanghai after reading the newspaper article about Sun in the weeks before his arrival. "What in the hell do we want with American generals?"[6]

When Sun and Lea finally arrived in Shanghai and a clandestine meeting of revolutionaries hurriedly arranged, Sun's fellow revolutionaries were reportedly shocked at the sight of Sun's hunchbacked companion, decked out in full military regalia; they were stunned at Sun's announcement of his plans to make Lea the chief commanding officer of the impending revolution. More than one of the men present at the meeting wondered if the leader of the new revolution in China had not temporarily gone mad. As the biographer of William Donald wrote with explicit, if politically incorrect, candor in later years, "Chinese people do not like deformed people in any circumstance, but for the leader of the revolution to have allied himself with a dwarf was, in their minds, beyond belief or excuse."[7]

Although Homer Lea had the potential to impact Chinese history and the revolution in unforeseen ways, his cool reception in Shanghai and his physical maladies continued to plague him until he was forced to return to the United States to seek medical treatment (he would die within a year of his return). What likely contributed most to Lea's downfall, however, was a critical decision made by Sun Yat-sen in regards to the future of the 1911 Revolution. It was a decision that left many of his followers again bewildered, and would have untold ramifications on Chinese history.

At the time of the October 10 Wuchang Uprising, the revolutionaries were in no way an organized and united military force. Far from it, the revolutionary movement consisted largely of very localized, ragtag factions of rebels having just one thing in common: the goal of bringing down the Manchu government. Very little thought was given to exactly what or who would replace the Qing government once it fell, however. It was commonly just assumed by the revolutionaries that anything would be better than the status quo, and that things would just naturally evolve once the corrupt and incompetent government in Beijing crumbled. The closer the reality of the fall of the Qing came, the more the folly of this lack of planning was realized.

The Qing government may have been rotten and corrupt, but it still had in it the primal urge to survive, and it wasn't about to go down without a fight. As a response to the impending revolution, it made one last desperate but dangerous decision. It went knocking on the door of a military official who had officially "retired" three years earlier after the mysterious death of Emperor Guangxu and the Empress Dowager Cixi, but who was in truth essentially exiled for fear of the threat he himself posed to the Qing government; he was the most experienced and powerful military leader in China at the time. The general was Yuan Shi Kai (袁世凱), and it was to him that the top-level Qing administrators pleaded for help in suppressing the ever-swelling revolution. Yuan immediately agreed to help.

Yuan was quick to recognize that the Qing government's days were numbered, and that if he played his cards right he himself could be the next leader of China. Realizing that a quick suppression of the Wuchang Uprising would render him essentially useless, Yuan negotiated with the revolutionaries instead of engaging them militarily. While the revolutionaries hastily elected Sun Yat-sen as the first president of the new Republic of China immediately after his return to China, Yuan effectively dismantled the Qing government by forcing the resignation of the boy Emperor Puyi and the Empress Dowager, replacing them with a cabinet he selected himself. So it was that this highest and proudest achievement of the revolutionary movement in China—the final abdication of the emperor—was not, as many had dreamed of, greeted with fireworks, parades, and stories of legendary heroics, but with a cataclysm of sloppy confusion mired in power grabs and politics. If the revolutionaries held any celebration at all in honor of the downfall of the Qing government and the establishment of a republic, it was a brief one. When negotiations with the revolutionaries resumed, Yuan was in a powerful position, and Sun Yat-sen and all of his followers knew it.

Sun Yat-sen was elected by his followers the provisional president of the newly established Republic of China in the days following his long-awaited return to China. The glory that Sun and Charlie basked in was as short-lived, however, as was his presidency. After Sun decided to base his new government in Nanjing, it quickly became apparent that Yuan Shi Kai was not about to step down from his position of power in Beijing; after Yuan agreed to force the formal abdication of the Emperor Puyi in exchange for the presidency of the Republic of China, it was all Sun could do to agree to step down and hand over the presidency to Yuan. By early April 1912, the Republic of China with Sun Yat-sen as president was dissolved as quickly as it was formed. Soon after his abdication, however, Sun wrote a letter to a friend, Li Xiao Sheng, which highlighted Charlie Soong's contribution to the revolutionary cause. It has remained one of the few artifacts in existence in which Sun Yat-sen directly acknowledges the nature of the contributions and sacrifices of Charlie Soong (Soong Jia Shu) in the name of the revolution.

> Soong Jia Shu, twenty years ago, together with me and Lu Haodong, discussed a revolution. For the last twenty years Soong Jia Shu has never waivered (sic). He never wanted fame or attention. Nevertheless, he contributed greatly to the revolution in Shanghai. He was involved with church and business activities on the surface, but secretly promoted the revolution as the "hermit of the revolution."[8]

Not only does the letter confirm that even Sun himself considered Charlie's low-key approach to revolution noteworthy, it proves that the relationship between Charlie and Sun remained strong in 1912 despite Sun's abdication of power. Charlie around this time even helped to arrange to send Sun's children to America for their education. It's not known how Charlie personally felt about Sun Yat-sen's decision to abdicate the presidency of the newly established Republic of China and formally recognize Yuan Shi Kai as president, and historians have debated ever since whether or not it was the best thing for Sun and his followers to do. On the one hand, immediate bloodshed was avoided and a largely peaceful transition of government ensued. Perhaps this was Sun's ultimate goal. If it was, then he succeeded and his unselfish refusal to be caught up in a power grab is commendable. On the other hand, many felt that Yuan Shi Kai was not fit to be president based upon his past actions, and that a government led by him would be just as corrupt, if not worse, than the Manchu government it just replaced. By acceding to his demands, Sun and his followers were only postponing the inevitable: a clash between Yuan's government and themselves. This, however, was not the only clash that was coming that Charlie Soong was unaware of. A confrontation of a far more personal nature was about to come crashing down upon him that would not only leave him shocked and bewildered, but cause him to question everything he thought he ever knew about the man who was to go down in history as the "Father of the Republic of China."

CHAPTER 12

FIRST CRACKS

———— ∞ ————

IF SUN'S YAT-SEN'S ULTIMATE GOAL was nothing more than to depose the emperor and topple the Manchu government in Beijing, then by 1912 his mission would have been considered a success. By avoiding confrontation with Yuan Shi Kai and agreeing to Yuan's demand for the office of the presidency of the newly established Republic of China, Sun hoped that his dream of a Chinese republic could avoid further bloodshed and get on with the business of formally and officially establishing itself both domestically and internationally. As part of the agreement between Yuan and Sun to end hostilities, Yuan was not the only one given a job to do, however. Sun was also assigned a new role and title in Yuan's new government. As the Director-General of Railway Development, he would be in charge of the nation's rapidly expanding railway network. While it was a legitimate posting, most historians have viewed it largely as a ploy by Yuan Shi Kai to placate Sun so that he would not be tempted to reorganize his followers and lead an attack on Yuan's new government. If this was Yuan's true goal, it worked—temporarily, anyway.

Just as important as Sun's decision to accept a position in Yuan's new government was the decision he made in regards to who he would bring with him to his new posting. He naturally

171

considered only his closest confidants and most trustworthy friends. That he chose Charlie Soong as the treasurer of his new venture came as no surprise to anyone. By 1912 Charlie's relationship with Sun dated back nearly two decades, and Charlie's service as treasurer of the revolutionary movement that finally culminated in the 1911 Revolution created a tight bond between the two men. What did perhaps come as a surprise to friends and family of Charlie Soong was his decision to accept the position.

Until now Charlie's tireless work in the service of the revolution was conducted entirely in secrecy. He went to great lengths to maintain his anonymity and make sure his revolutionary activities stayed covert. His methods and tactics were well thought out and ultimately successful up to and through the Revolution of 1911. Both he and his family remained free of any suspicion for nearly two decades, and because of his discreet diligence both he and they stayed out of harm's way. His decision to accept Sun's invitation to be treasurer of the railroad venture, however, completely transformed his life overnight. The anonymity he had enjoyed in previous years evaporated, and with it the guarantee of safety. No one at the time knew what lay in Sun Yat-sen's future, or the future of China, but for now Charlie Soong was making a very public bet that Dr. Sun was worth following, and that the time was right for publicly coming out in support of him. The first photograph ever taken of Charlie standing together with Sun Yat-sen and a small group of other advisors and directors in 1912 was intended to be a token of celebration and appreciation in honor of all the men who were so faithful to Sun Yat-sen and his revolutionary cause. Sun's enemies, however, would soon use such photographs for an entirely different purpose.

Charlie wasn't the only Soong that would be following Sun to the railway venture. Charlie's oldest daughter Ai-ling, now in her early twenties, was appointed Sun's secretary. The three of them, and "an assortment of others," formed the tightknit group that was to become Sun's advisors and associates during his brief tenure as director of the railway venture. Although he based his operations in Shanghai, the job put him on the road a great majority of the time, mostly on board trains traveling to far-flung regions of China that had yet to fully develop their railway networks. It was not a particularly glamorous job, but it was made palatable by the fact that he was able to travel on the Empress Dowager's old train, luxuriously appointed and eminently more comfortable than any ordinary train car. While traveling across the country, the train would stop at towns and cities along the way where Sun would make speeches, meet with officials, and announce plans for building local railway lines. It was in the railway headquarters back in Shanghai, however, after an otherwise uneventful tour of the country, that Charlie Soong's long relationship with Sun Yat-sen was about to take its first direct hit.

According to Donald, the Australian reporter who was rapidly becoming Sun's closest confidant, the incident took place after Ai-ling Soong, in the midst of secretarial duties, left Sun's office where the two men were discussing affairs of the day. In a calm and collected voice, Sun looked across the table at Donald and "whispered that he wanted to marry her," a desire that Donald advised him to quickly sublimate not only because he was already married, but because Ai-ling was more than two decades younger and the daughter of one of his closest friends.[1]

"I know it," Dr. Sun said. "I know it. But I want to marry her just the same."

Dr. Sun persisted until he convinced Donald to accompany him to Soong's house that very night, where he "intended to petition the father to permit the marriage."

According to Donald, Charlie "met Sun's request as if the little doctor had struck him a stupefying blow." Immediately afterwards, the "color drained from his cheeks, and he looked haggardly at the man by whose side he had stood for nearly twenty years." Charlie, at a loss for words, eventually summoned up a response intended to remind Sun of his religion and his values and dismiss the proposal outright.

"Yat-sen, I am a Christian man. All the time, I thought you were, too. I did not bring up my children to live in the sort of looseness that you propose. I will not accustom myself to people who trifle with marriage. We are a Christian family and, Lord willing, we will go on that way."

The three men sat in awkward silence, with Charlie stunned, Sun embarrassed, and Donald wishing he were anywhere else but where he was. Charlie, still recovering from the shock, eventually roused up enough gumption to get in the last word. "I want you to go, and I never want you to come back," he firmly and resolutely told Sun. "My door is closed to you forever."

It's difficult to say what cut deeper into the heart of Charlie Soong more after this painfully awkward and unquestionably inappropriate exchange of words between him and Dr. Sun. If it wasn't the sudden and unexpected end to what he likely considered one of the most treasured and valuable friendships in his entire life, it was certainly the unanticipated questioning of the leadership of the revolution to which his life had been dedicated for nearly two decades. If the values of the man who was leading the revolution were now suddenly called into question, what of the purpose and aim of the revolution itself? Whatever the answer, it was clear that Charlie Soong's long-cherished relationship with Sun Yat-sen would never be the same.

Much to the dismay of both men, the marriage proposal incident between Sun and Soong that marked the beginning of the end of their friendship could not be neatly filtered out of their work relationship. Regardless of the increasing unease between them, they still had a job to do, and they still had a common goal. Despite the ever-growing divide between them, however, they were about to be thrown into a situation that would force them to work together more closely than ever before.

Just as the Chinese Revolution of 1911 did not have a clean beginning, it also did not have a clean ending. For several months after the Wuchang Uprising in October of 1911, it was not clear who the new leader of China was, especially since Sun Yat-sen was nowhere to be found. The power struggle that eventually formed between Sun and Yuan Shi Kai ultimately resulted in Yuan becoming China's new president in the spring of 1912, but with an agreement between all parties to hold elections later in the year to formally and democratically elect the new "official" leader of China. Almost predictably, however, when the time came to hold elections, Yuan Shi Kai not only hesitated to relinquish power, but arranged the assassination of his number one opponent in the Kuomintang (KMT), the political party organized by Sun Yat-sen several years earlier. Indeed, the brutal assassination in March 1913 of Song Jiaoren (宋教仁), the favored KMT candidate to win the presidency of the still nascent Republic of China, was the final straw in the increasingly bitter conflict between Sun Yat-sen's KMT party and Yuan Shi Kai. In a matter of days after the assassination of Song Jiaoren, the Second Revolution was officially underway.

The Second Revolution brought violence and uprisings back to China almost as quickly as they disappeared in the wake of the 1911 Revolution. This time it was the forces of Yuan

Shi Kai against the loose amalgamation of KMT forces that rose up in opposition to him. In the wake of the new outbreak of violence, Sun Yat-sen was immediately re-branded an outlaw by Yuan's government. As a result, it was eventually considered too risky for him to remain in Shanghai, and he subsequently fled to Japan. This time, however, he would not be alone, for now Charlie Soong was clearly and publicly associated with both Sun and the revolution as a result of their work together at the train bureau. And Charlie, along with the rest of his family that were in Shanghai at the time (May-ling and T. V. were attending college in America), was forced to go along. The safety and security that Charlie and his family enjoyed for two decades as a result of his anonymity were now a distant memory, and the danger that could be contained in the past now erupted with a fury. Japan would be their new home, but no one knew for how long—a month, a year, a decade, or forever. It had now been over twenty-five years since Charlie Soong lived abroad. And now, this time with a family in tow, he was about to do so again.

In the fall of 1914, nearly a year after Charlie's arrival in Japan, the same missionary who was with Charlie in Shanghai the day after the Wuchang Uprising was traveling back to Shanghai after spending a sabbatical year in America. Coincidentally, she ran into him at a Tokyo train station.

> I was standing in the station in Tokyo, with my little daughter asleep on my shoulder, waiting while Mr. Roberts bought our tickets to Yokohama. I felt two arms encircle me and some one said 'And this is your tiny baby?' I exclaimed, 'Why, Mr. Soong, whatever are you doing here?' 'Don't say my name too loud,' he cautioned,

and then with his old chuckle, 'Would you like to make fifty thousand? That's what Yuan Shi-Kai values my poor old head at. Let's sit down and I'll tell you all about it.' So he told us of Yuan's plotting and how he had been forced to take refuge in Japan, because Yuan knew he was a friend of Sun's. In the few minutes until our train left, we tried to cram all the questions we wanted to ask and all that he had to tell us. As our train pulled out, he stood waving to us, with his eyes full of tears, and never have I hated more to leave anyone.[2]

The recollection of the missionary regarding her unexpected reunion with Charlie offers a glimpse of the lighthearted and humorous part of his personality that was so evident during his time in North Carolina, but it also highlights the fact that he still considered himself in much danger in Japan. Nearly a year after the encounter at the train station, however, a letter written by Charlie himself began to indicate a danger increasingly facing him, one of an entirely different nature. The letter was written by Charlie to his son T. V., who was at college in America.

Chinese Y.M.C.A.
Tokio, May 3rd, 1915

My dear Son,

I am very sorry to tell you that I cannot come to see you and Mayling as I expected and decided to do. I have had frequent headache and eye trouble and recently by accident I discovered that my right eye is almost totally blind. I went to see a specialist on eye discease and after examined me for fully an hour he said I had kidney trouble (Bright's discease). I went to see a famous specialist in the Imperial University of Tokio and he too told me that I have the kidney trouble. I again went to see an English doctor at St. Luke's hospital of Tokio and he also said I have chronic kidney trouble and advised me to live on milk and fruit only for a month and he said I must take good care of myself or the discease may get the upperhand of me.

Please let Mayling see this for I shall not write another similar letter one will do for you both. I shall remain here two weeks longer and then leave for Kobe where I expect to spend my summer at least.

If you would like to see me you may get a return ticket and come to Japan to spend the summer with me. If Mayling wishes to come with you may make the same arrangement for her to come along—But you <u>must arrange</u> with the immigration officer at the port of either San Francisco or Seattle so that when you return to school at next the fall you will have no trouble landing on U.S. soil. I think you had better get your ticket to Kobe and back for it will not cost anymore than to Yokohama and back. I think Mayling says during the Panama Exposition the passage between Japan and America is cheaper than usual and I think you ought to bring Mayling with for I do not know whether I shall be able to live long enough until she graduates. The nature of my sickness is not certain. It may carry me away very quickly and I wish to see you both before I die. I shall ask mother, Rosa, John and Josey to come over to Japan to see you both—

My cable address is "Soong Kobe". So please cable me if you and Mayling are coming you signify: "Coming". But if <u>you</u> are coming alone they say: "Come", and I will understand. Rosa has been in Tokio over a month and Eling came after her and stayed with me for three weeks. I sent them both home, today—They will sail for Shanghai on board French mail steamer "Vera" on the 6th and expect to be at home on the 10th. God bless you both. Don't forget the necessary papers from the American immigration officer to fecilitate your relanding on American soil when you return to school.[3]

With love to you both—
I am your most Affectionate father
C.J. Soong

As Charlie indicated, he was hoping for yet one more trip back to America. His health, however, forced him to make other plans. The diagnosis of Bright's Disease, an inflammation of the kidneys more commonly known today as chronic nephritis, did not bode well for his future. Only in his mid-fifties, Charlie was now quite cognizant of his mortality, and had no problem expressing his sentiments in this regard in his painfully honest letter. If the diagnosis of Bright's Disease was accurate, his eye problems would eventually be accompanied by back pain, vomiting, high blood pressure, and severe edema. Only time would tell how long it would be before those symptoms began appearing. In a second letter to his son, written only three months after the first, Charlie goes on to further detail developments in the condition of his health, and provide details regarding everyday events in his life.

Chinese Club
24 Nanayamate Dinsan chome
Kobe, August 6th 1915

My dear son,

Your post card sent from Burlington came with Mayling's letter by the same mail. I am glad to know you are both in good health. Take good care of it. Without a good health an education is practically as worthless to the possession as well as to others. Therefore, always keep your eye on your health above all things.

Shanghai has experienced the greatest storm in her history recently. Mother says she never saw such a storm in Shanghai before. All the trees on the B____ were blown down. All the boats and sampans in the river were blown on shore. Our high galvanized iron screen was blown down and crushed on New's "feapo" tree and broke it. A coasting steamer named "Chintai" was overturned bottomup near Woosung with over 200 passengers on board and over 100 were drown on the spot. There were four girls who recently returned from American colleges were on board and drown among the passengers. It is so sad to think about such tragedy. They had escaped danger of the ocean and yet were made victims of their native river without ever a glimpse of their parents.

Old Uncle Chang's daughter is about to be married to a man who is earning $120 per month. Aunt _eio is the Match maker. Singdo is about to be married also to a man who earns something like $200 or $300 per month. Liu Keng is now a chief clerk of British & American tobacco company in Tientsin. He gets$195 per month and is negotiating for a wife. Kway Yung Giang is dead & his wife is a hades to his mother Zung(.) Zung Giang was a dutiful son before his marriage but after marriage he was a veritable villain, and because he listened to his wife and treated his mother so badly while he was living after his death his wife treats his mother even worse.

How ungrateful some people do turned out to be!

Wu Kaim Oh is in Japan. He brought his two daughters with hom. One is 12 yrs. old and the other is 10.

They are staying with their distant relative at Tarumi, a seashore resort. It is about 3/4 hour's ride by train from Kobe. This relative of their is Mr. Y.K. Pow assistant compradore of Yokohama Spice Bank of Kobe. I was also know him. Kaimoh called at the club to see me and said Mr. Pow invited me to go down to spend a day with hime so I went down with him the same afternoon(.) Kaimoh is going to Stami & Tokio on Saturday and will return to China on the 20th of this month. Kaimoh has the stomach trouble.

Yesterday I met LiTsing liang on the road with other Chinese students who were introduced to me as doctor so and so both of them. They are going to the U.S.A. to take a special course of study. I understand Le Tsing Meur is also in U.S.A. He went there last December.

Mother is going to Shansi to see Eling next month as E. is expected to be confined then. I wrote Chingling a long letter & requested her to accompany mother there & back but she seems to want to remain in Shanghai and asked me to go with mother. I would be willing to go if it is perfectly safe for me to do so. But if I go I still wish her to go along with us. I wrote to her again & said that if it is perfectly safe for me to go I will but she must go with us to keep up company and be a comfort to us. And if she is willing to comply with my request then cable me & I will return by first steamer. So I am waiting for a reply from her.

I am improving in health thank god. But there is still albumen in my urine and my blood pressure is very high yet.

Perhaps this is the last letter I write to you from Kobe and if I get the reply next week I shall leave for home at once. Congratulate you upon the highest honour co-ferred on you by the students in America.[4]

With love to you both
Yr loving father
C.J. Soong

There is much of interest in Charlie's second letter to his son in America, not the least of which is his interest in the monthly salaries of friends and acquaintances. More importantly, howev-er, Charlie revealed that his wife was now living back in Shanghai, where she returned before Charlie on account of health-related issues of her own. It was apparently deemed safe for her and the rest of the family to return to Shanghai, but Charlie decided to wait it out a bit longer. His repeated use of the phrase "if it is per-fectly safe for me to do so" is indicative of his extreme caution regarding his decision to move back to China. It is also a curios-ity that Charlie's next-door neighbor in Shanghai is named New, leading to speculation that his neighbor was also his brother-in-law and longtime friend from his Boston childhood days, S. C. New. It is the last few paragraphs of the letter, however, that would prove most relevant to Charlie's future. The stubbornness and refusal of his second daughter, Ching-ling, to accompany her mother to Shansi to help her sister Ai-ling (while in Japan in 1914, Ai-ling married H. H. Kung, a wealthy young Chinese man from a prominent Chinese family that could trace its roots back to Confucius) with the birth and care of her first child was a foreshadowing of things to come.

CHAPTER 13

SURPRISE ENDINGS

───⊸∞⊶───

SOMETIME IN THE FALL OF 1915 Charlie Soong deemed his situation safe enough to finally merit returning to Shanghai to rejoin his wife and family. Yuan Shi Kai was still officially in power in Beijing, but his reign was weakening by the day. His decision to appoint himself the new emperor of China late in 1915 all but sealed his fate. Chinese everywhere were still not quite sure what or who their leader should be, but they were generally unanimous in one regard: that their next leader would not be an emperor. Opposition to Yuan and his rule gained momentum by the day in the closing weeks of 1915, and the fact that Yuan's days were numbered was obvious to everyone but Yuan himself.

When Charlie returned to Shanghai late in the fall of 1915, his wife was already in Shansi to help their daughter, Ai-ling, with the birth and care of their first child. It's not known whether Charlie and Ching-ling ever went to Shansi at all to help Ai-ling and Mrs. Soong. It is distinctly possible that Charlie remained in Shanghai to keep an eye on Ching-ling, and that his reason for doing so was based on an almost instinctual fear of what was about to transpire. Details vary about exactly what happened, but there has been little argument about its profound impact not only on the Soong family, but also on Chinese history itself.

Ching-ling had graduated from Wesleyan College in 1913. Upon her graduation, instead of returning to China like she had long anticipated, she was forced to go to Japan where here mother and father were in temporary, self-imposed exile. While there, she naturally mingled with other Chinese, as well as the Chinese revolutionaries there at the time. Despite the fact that she was still just shy of twenty years old upon her arrival in Japan, Ching-ling's personality was well-developed and stood in stark contrast to that of her sisters. Every Chinese today can recite the phrase that succinctly encapsulated their personalities. Of the Soong sisters, it is commonly said, "One loved power, one loved money, and one loved China." Of all her brothers and sisters, Ching-ling is said to have been the most intense in regards to her sincerity of purpose and political fervor. So it was that in the wake of her sister Ai-ling's decision to marry in 1914, Ching-ling was duly appointed the new secretary to Sun Yat-sen. The post of secretary to Sun Yat-sen did not last long (less than a year), however, and it is unknown why. Speculation exists that her post as Sun Yat-sen's secretary was long enough in duration for her and Sun to develop a relationship that superseded the boundaries of any ordinary workplace relationship, and that suspicion of a mutual attraction between Sun and Ching-ling even influenced Charlie to send Ching-ling back to Shanghai with his wife at least a year before Charlie himself decided to return to China. Regardless, by early 1915, Ching-ling was living back in Shanghai with her mother.

Charlie, too, moved back to Shanghai in the early fall of 1915 after deeming that it was once again safe for him to return to China, but it was on an October night that Mrs. Soong returned from her extended visit with Ai-ling in Shansi that events took their fateful turn for both the Soongs and for China's future.

It wasn't until a few months later, in a letter written by a friend of H. H. Kung's (Ai-ling's new husband) to G. E. Morrison, an Australian journalist turned Chinese government political advisor after the establishment of the Republic of China, that details of the fateful night were revealed. In the letter, Ai-ling is referred to as "Mrs. K'ung," Mr. K'ung is Ai-ling's husband, and Ching-ling is referred to by her English name, Rosamond (the name bestowed in honor of the daughter of the Wilmington, North Carolina, mentor of Charlie's, Reverend Ricaud).

792. From R.R. Gailey

Peking 12 December 1915

Dear Dr. Morrison,

This is not the first time I have written to you when Chinese in whom I am interested were in trouble, or in danger of getting involved unjustly. It is the memory of your sympathy and promise of aid if necessary which prompts me to write again, though I hope that in this case there will be no need of intervention. I want you to be informed in regard to Mr. K'ung so that if any emergency should arise, there would be no delay in getting necessary information.

Mr. K'ung tried twice to see you during his recent stay in Peking, but you were not at home. He wishes to acquaint you with the facts of this enclosed statement. Whether he would have told you in addition of recent family complications I do not know, but because of the investigations of this detective I think it is well to tell you, though Mr. K'ung told me in confidence. Mrs. K'ung has a younger sister, Rosamonde, who has recently returned from study in America. This impulsive girl has been enticed by Dr. Sun to marry him, his wife having been divorced for this purpose. This daughter was with her father in Shanghai, her mother having gone to Shansi to be with her daughter Mrs. K'ung in her confinement. The night that her mother returned to Shanghai the girl left for Japan with an emissary of Dr. Sun who had been sent there for her. Her parents were distressed beyond measure, and as soon as they could get a clue of their daughter's whereabouts, they followed her to Japan, but arrived too late, the marriage having already taken place. It was distress at this which caused Mr. Sung's (Soong's) serious illness, and called his daughter, Mrs. K'ung to his bedside at Chingdao (Tsingtao). The family feel very bitter against Dr. Sun for enticing this innocent enthusiastic daughter of an old friend to leave her home in this clandestine mélange, also for his faithlessness to the wife who had shared his trials, and whose children are older than the girl whom he recently married.

If you think this statement should be shown to Dr. Reinsch, will you inform him, or send to him yourself? I do not know whether he is acquainted with Mr. K'ung.[1]

Yours sincerely,
[R.R. Gailey]

As the letter states, Sun sent an "emissary" to Shanghai to secretly pick up Ching-ling and accompany her back to Japan. The whole affair was apparently planned well in advance and Ching-ling simply waited for an opportune time to execute the plan.

The fact that Charlie and his wife were "distressed beyond measure" is perhaps an understatement. Not only was their daughter in the midst of eloping overseas, but she was also eloping with one of her father's best friends, a man nearly three decades her senior. Furthermore, Sun Yat-sen was already married, and the Soongs were friends with his wife just as they were friends with him. What upset and alarmed Charlie and Mrs. Soong the most as both Christians and parents, however, was their almost certain knowledge of Sun Yat-sen's proclivities; prior to Sun's marriage to Ching-ling, he was not only married, but was known to have had relationships with other women while married, including Chen Cuifen (often referred to in history as "Sun Yat-sen's concubine" and "The Forgotten Revolutionary Female"), and although somewhat less substantiated, Kaoru Otsuki, a Japanese girl whom Sun allegedly first met in 1898 and married just four years later while Kaoru was still a teenager. Charlie Soong was certainly as aware of this as anyone. While it was not uncommon for wealthy and powerful Chinese men of prior eras to take on multiple girlfriends and wives, such behavior was anathema to the Soongs. The mere thought of their own daughter, whom they took great pains to educate overseas and raise according to the strict principles of their religion, marrying an older divorcé and potentially becoming what was tantamount to a concubine was certainly nearly as devastating as a death in the family for Charlie and his wife.

The Soongs' trip to Japan to stop the marriage was hard on Charlie, whose health was already severely compromised by kidney disease. The fact that he was too late to Japan to stop the marriage only exacerbated his ill health, to the point where he was bedridden in Qingdao en route back to Shanghai. That the Soong family felt "very bitter against

Dr. Sun" was more than likely an understatement. Indeed, if Charlie thought that Sun was finished pursuing his daughters after the embarrassing incident two years prior in which Sun asked Charlie for Ai-ling's hand in marriage, he was mistaken. The pain and bitterness that stemmed from that incident came roaring back with a vengeance after Ching-ling's sudden trip to Japan to marry Sun. Charlie Soong had always wanted revolution since his return to China nearly thirty years before, but the cost of the revolution was beginning to take a toll on him that he never possibly could have prepared for or anticipated.

An enclosure in the letter to G. E. Morrison meant to provide some background on the relationship between Sun Yat-sen, the Soongs, and now H. H. Kung provides further evidence of the discord that increasingly existed between Sun Yat-sen and the Soongs. The excerpt begins with a reference to the 1914 marriage between Charlie's daughter Ai-ling, whom Sun wanted to marry just three years before, and H. H. K'ung.

Enclosure to letter No. 792: Statement in regard to Mr. &
Mrs. H.H. K'ung

...Dr. Sun did not favor this marriage. Mr. K'ung had never identified himself with the revolutionists, though offers had been made to him, and Dr. Sun doubtless felt that he might some time need again the services of his former very efficient secretary. For this and other reasons the break between Dr. Sun and the Sung family has been complete of late, and the old friendship has become an enmity. The Sung family returned to Shanghai. An important family affair, having no connection with politics, took Mr. Sung to Japan recently. He got back to Ching'tao ill, and Mrs. K'ung was summoned there from Shansi. He has since improved in health and returned to Shanghai...[2]

According to the letter, if there was anything left of the relationship between Charlie and Sun, it evaporated completely when Ai-ling married H. H. Kung. One can speculate whether it was truly Sun's dislike and distrust of Kung or simple jealousy over Ai-ling's marriage that caused his ultimate break with the Soongs, but it doesn't matter. Sun Yat-sen, now a divorcé, had eloped with the daughter of his longtime friend, Charlie Soong. Ultimately, Sun's decision to secretly marry Ching-ling during a fractious time in his relationship with Charlie acted as a final dagger in the back of their friendship.

Charlie and Mrs. Soong weren't the only ones stunned by the marriage of their daughter to Sun Yat-sen. It took a few months, but news of the scandal eventually spread overseas, and the Christian communities who had previously been so vocal and active in their support of Sun Yat-sen and his revolutionary cause were equally shocked and dismayed. The news was difficult to fathom. Sun Yat-sen had claimed to be a Christian all these years; now he was not only divorced, but he had eloped with the daughter of one of his closest friends. When rumors of the marriage were confirmed, Sun not surprisingly lost face in the international community, especially among Christians. The case has been made that his behavior irreparably damaged both his reputation and the reputation of his world-famous revolutionary movement.

The fall of Yuan Shi Kai in China was accompanied by a sense of karmic justice, for in the same stealthy manner he brutally inserted himself into China's highest political office, his rapid decline came about as the result of his own corrupt and incompetent leadership. The sign of ultimate hubris that signaled his imminent demise came with his decision to declare himself the new emperor of China; by the time of his death in June 1916 he was largely impotent as regional rulers began superseding his authority. Unfortunately, the leaders that succeeded Yuan were little better than him and China plunged into a decades-long period of radical instability. A parade of warlords filled the leadership vacuum left by Yuan after he died, and the presidency of the fledgling Republic of China for more than a decade was most characterized by a revolving door.

China in 1916 was certainly not in possession of the model of republican government that Sun Yat-sen or Charlie Soong envisioned for so long, and for a short while it almost looked as if dynastic rule might return to China. Both Sun and Soong retained their optimism, however, even if the circumstances of the day gave them no reason to. The year 1917 did not bring more stability to China, nor did it restore health or vitality to an increasingly frail Charlie Soong. While much of the rest of the world was mired in the muck of World War I, however, it did bring a refreshing and invigorating reunion with one of the most loved, respected, and admired figures in Charlie's life. After Charlie's recent experiences with Sun Yat-sen, it was a reunion that could not have come at a better time.

Julian Carr, Charlie's benefactor and lifelong friend back in Durham, North Carolina, turned seventy-two in 1917. When he decided to make a round-the-world trip to Asia, it did not surprise anyone. His vigor and enthusiasm certainly were not what they were when he acted as mentor and benefactor to Charlie Soong during his youthful and formative North Carolina years, but they still existed in abundance. His wife's death a few years prior profoundly affected him, but his stamina remained unabated. The trip to Asia was possibly arranged to assuage his loneliness in the wake of his wife's death, but it was officially made in order to help one of the many organizations that Carr had associated with during his long life.

Since Charlie left America in the mid-1880s, Julian Carr's life continued to unfold like a classic American novel, complete with a rags-to-riches (and eventually back to rags) storyline. Soon after Charlie's departure from North Carolina, Carr built a new house in Durham that became the talk of the town for decades to come for its opulence and grandeur. His tobacco company shot to the top of the industry for several years only to eventually succumb to fierce competition. The American Tobacco Company, the quasi-monopoly formed by Durham tobacco magnate Washington Duke, was particularly instrumental in the downfall of Carr's tobacco company (and would go on to be one of the first twelve companies listed on the Dow Jones Industrial Average). In collaboration with his business arch-nemesis, however, Carr was a primary force in the establishment of Duke University. It was Julian Carr's generous donation of his private land that allowed Trinity College to move from the tiny town of Trinity, North Carolina, to Durham, where the college would eventually change its name to Duke University in honor of Washington Duke.

Without missing a beat, Carr made the successful transition from the tobacco business to the textile business at a time when the America South was becoming a major player in the world textile market. Carr's penchant for involving himself in grand causes of all kinds also remained as fervent as ever as he got older, and his popularity in and around Durham never waned. In 1900 he was even named a candidate for vice-president of the United States by North Carolina delegates at the Democratic National Convention. Later the town of Carrboro, North Carolina, would eventually be named in honor of him and his decision to help bring electricity to the town to help facilitate the development of a textile industry. Finally, two years after the death of his wife, at the request of the American Honorary Commercial Commission, Carr accepted an invitation to travel to Asia to "help promote closer trade relations between the United States and the Orient."

Carr's Asian tour in the spring of 1917 would take him to various destinations in the region. After taking a train to the West Coast and departing from Vancouver on the *Empress of Russia*, his journey to Japan was plagued by cold weather and snowstorms, causing many on the ship to fall victim to seasickness (Carr wrote proudly in his diary that he was not among them). Following a stopover in Yokahama, Japan, he would sail to the Philippines and attend a banquet organized by the Manila Merchants Association. In a letter written to the *Morning Herald* in Durham, he spoke highly of Manila, but was somewhat put off by the reaction to a speech he gave to them that praised President Wilson, a speech for which he "failed to receive a single handclap."[3]

Afterwards sailing to Hong Kong, he continued to Canton, where he was greeted and entertained by high-level government officials and "dined at the Palace with the Governor, the Chief Justice of the Supreme Court and his wife & other members of the Governor's Council...a distinguished body of Chinese gentlemen." After continuing on to Beijing, where he met with a committee of local bankers, he visited a local school, saw the

Great Wall of China, and finally set sail for Shanghai on the *S.S. Siberia*. At 10 p.m. on the evening of Wednesday, March 21, 1917, Julian Carr reached Shanghai, and standing there ever faithful in friendship to greet him at the docks was none other than his old friend and one-time dependent, Charlie Soong.[4]

Carr kept a diary of his time in Shanghai. Unfortunately, it is little more than a log of names, dates, and places. It does, however, provide some insight into the schedule and activities of Carr during his visit, and most of the time he was in the company of Charlie. On the night of his arrival, he was booked into the Burlington Hotel, one of the high-end hotels catering to foreigners in Shanghai at the time, where, he writes, he was registered as "the guest of Charlie Soon." The day after his arrival, he visited a kindergarten with Charlie and had lunch with the principal. A few days later, he traveled two and a half hours to Soochow (苏州), where he was the "Guest of Dr. and Mrs. Park," and gave a local kindergarten fifty dollars (donations and precise amounts are one of the few things Carr kept strict track of in his diary). Charlie also accompanied him on this trip. From Soochow, the two men headed to Song Jiang (松江), where they visited friends and acquaintances, returning to Shanghai on the evening of March 28. A few days later, it was back to Soochow again for a visit to the Soochow University Bible School and Charlie's Vanderbilt classmate, William Burke, who was still a missionary in Song Jiang.

In Burke's biography a brief reference to this visit states that Charlie and Carr "visited Shanghai on a pleasure trip...to spend a day with Burke," but that, "the little Chinese looked ill..." Even more poignantly, it also documents the only known time Charlie ever mentioned anything to anyone regarding the deep disappointment he felt over the scandal involving Sun Yat-sen and his daughter. "I was never so hurt in my life," he told Burke in a rare display of raw emotion during the visit. "My own daughter and my best friend."[5]

On Saturday, March 31, 1917, while in Song Jiang, Carr wrote of "a great reception attended by a great crowd," likely given in his honor, which members of the Ministry of Education, Agriculture, and the Board of Trade attended. The following evening, Carr noted simply that he "spoke 3 times," presumably to religious congregations at the invite of their leaders since it was a Sunday (the Reverends Bowman, Patterson, and Burke are listed). In the evening he and Charlie again returned to Shanghai.

On Thursday, April 5, Carr left Shanghai on the ship *Shingo Maru*. "Several friends came down (to) the ship with me," he fondly recalled later. Present at Carr's farewell on the docks of Shanghai were Charlie and his family members, who had brought along a gift: a set of three large meticulously painted Chinese porcelain vases neatly packaged and clearly addressed to Carr's home in Durham (one of these vases still survives today at the University of North Carolina at Chapel Hill).

It was good timing on Julian Carr's part to visit Charlie when he did, for it was obvious to William Burke that Charlie looked ill when Carr and Charlie visited him in 1917. As Charlie certainly expected, the kidney disease that first started giving him trouble in Japan back in 1915 progressed until it eventually sent him to the hospital in Shanghai. After Charlie's daughter May-ling returned to China in 1917, after studying nearly a decade in America, letters written by her to a college friend in America provide the only known firsthand account of Charlie's last days. Those days, according to May-ling, were not pleasant.

By April 1918 Charlie was rapidly losing both strength and weight. He was increasingly bloated and his skin began drying out so badly that May-ling resorted to giving him "a massage with olive oil to soothe his dry, parchment-like skin." After a short hospital stay, his wife insisted that Charlie come home since it was clear that death was imminent. May-ling, frustrated at her mother's lack of belief in modern medicine, resorted to emoting in a letter to her American friend. "Mother says she does not believe in doctors, and that no one could cure him but God. Hence, she refuses to let him be sweated to throw off the poison. I am frantic...as his kidneys are not working. I am almost going crazy with the tension and Mother's refusal to follow the doctor's direction. He sleeps most of the time, and his face is swollen. I believe in prayer, but I also believe in medicine."[6] May-ling's pain and her frustration with her father's situation would not last. On May 4, 1918, the man known to the world as Charlie Soong died at the age of fifty-six at his home in Shanghai, China.

There was nothing unusual about Charlie Soong's "quiet and simple funeral," with the perhaps not-so-curious absence of Sun Yat-sen, who was now also living in Shanghai. There were "only close friends and relatives in attendance." What was interesting was Charlie's own decision to be buried in the International Cemetery, "a new burial ground in Shanghai for well-to-do Chinese and foreigners." According to May-ling, "Father was the very first person to be buried in that cemetery. He liked being the first in any kind of competition; he would be awfully pleased." Perhaps Charlie also never forgot his time in Massachusetts, North Carolina, and Tennessee, and that his experiences there contributed to a truly international identity.

As an indication that North Carolina also never forgot about Charlie, the following obituary appeared in the *Wilmington Dispatch* in Wilmington, North Carolina, on July 5, 1918, two months after Charlie's death, under the headline "Notable

Career of Chinese Youth Ends." Although some of the details regarding Charlie's life (particularly in regards to his children) are incorrect, it does not detract from the communal sentiment expressed.

Unusual local interest attaches to the death of Rev. Charles Jones Soong, which occurred in Shanghai on May 4 from Bright's disease, according to a communication received by General Julian S. Carr, of Durham, because it was here that the climb upward of Dr. Soong, known locally as Charlie Soong, was begun. The first helping hand stretched out to the little Chinese boy who later amassed a fortune and rose to high position was the hand of a Wilmington man—Rev. T. Page Ricaud, at that time pastor of the Fifth Avenue Methodist church, and father of Addison G. Ricaud, prominent member of the local bar.

There are many here who remember Charlie Soong, who was employed as a cook aboard the old side wheel revenue cutter COLFAX at the age of 17. That was back in the early 1880s. The youth was intensely interested in things religious, and his constant attendance upon services at the Fifth Avenue church attracted the attention and kindled the interest of Dr. Ricaud, who later interested General Carr in the boy. His position was resigned aboard the cutter, and he was installed in the palatial home of General Carr in Durham. His education was paid for by the Trinity Sunday school of Durham and he was prepared for entrance to Vanderbilt university with the object of preparing him for the ministry. Following the completion of his education he went abroad and became private secretary to a high Chinese official, amassing a fortune and rising rapidly in the world, becoming one of the leading men in Shanghai. On his return to Shanghai he married the daughter of a native missionary and reared a family of five children—three girls and two boys. Four of the children have already been educated in this country, and the fifth was prepared to enter Harvard University was to have come to the United States in September. The three girls received diplomas from Wesleyan Female college, Macon, Ga. The two eldest, Virginia Lee and Rosamonde, returned to China after graduation; the youngest, Mayling, chose to go to Wellesly college and take a post-graduate course, from which institution she graduated just a year ago. General Carr on his return from China brought in his baggage a white silk gown that was sent by Mayling's parents for her graduating exercises. This young girl came to America when she was nine years old and entered Wesleyan Female college, returning to China at the age of 19 and taking with her two diplomas, one from Wesleyan Female college and the other from Wellesly college, Massachusetts. The oldest son graduated from Harvard and then took a post-graduate course at Columbia university, returning home at the same time with his sister, carrying with him two diplomas, one from Harvard and the other from Columbia. The youngest boy was graduated from the University of Shanghai and expects to enter Harvard at the fall term.

When General Carr was in the Orient some 18 months ago, it was a great pleasure to him to visit the home and family of his former protégée, Charlie Soong. His second daughter, Rosamonde, was the wife of the first president of the Republic of China, and General Carr believes she was the handsomest young woman he saw in China. The oldest daughter, Virginia Lee, was married to Dr. Kuhn, who is president of a college of high grade and of more than 400 students up near Peking, the capital of China. Dr. Sun Yat Sen, the husband of Rosamonde, was perhaps the first man in China. In fact, the former consul general of the United States, Hon. Thomas J. Jernigan, appointed under the Cleveland administration, in a conversation with General Carr, pronounced Dr. Sun the first citizen of China. Certainly this was an instance of "casting bread upon the waters."[7]

Charles Jones Soong likely did not live as long as he would have preferred, nor did the revolution he helped bring about bear the fruit of his ultimate vision. His contributions to China and its future, however, were as profound and far-reaching as they were underappreciated in the twentieth century, and will continue to exist long after his passing. His pro-industrialization views, though now common in China, were characteristic of a man ahead of his time. His uncelebrated role as an education advocate, particularly in regards to women's education, was also far ahead of his time. Most of all, his uncompromising vision in regards to China and its unrealized potential, was a vision for which he was willing to sacrifice everything that meant anything to him.

CHAPTER 14

LEGACIES

∞∞∞

I T'S NOT UNUSUAL FOR CHILDREN to be more famous than their parents, or vice versa. In Charlie Soong's case, it would be several of his children who would go on to achieve a fame that he never could have imagined, nor would have likely desired.

Charlie's youngest daughter, May-ling, achieved a degree of fame in the United States that no Chinese had before. There were some Chinese before her that gained notoriety in America, but none ever approached the level of popularity that May-ling did in the years before and after World War II. Her marriage to Chiang Kai-shek (蔣介石) in the 1920s, after which she was typically referred to as Madame Chiang Kai-shek, catapulted her name into international stardom when Chiang himself arose to the top echelon of military and political power in China in the 1930s and 1940s. It was overlooked by no one that when he married Soong May-ling, he was also marrying the sister of the wife of Sun Yat-sen, his own personal mentor and the closest thing the Chinese had to a national hero.

During World War II Chinese diplomats had a difficult time convincing the rest of the world community of China's dire situation and of their need for support in their war against the Japanese. Someone who could relate equally well to both

Chinese and Americans was of potentially tremendous value to the Chinese cause. So it was that May-ling Soong, with her fluent English and her American university education, fit the role of China's de facto ambassador better than any official in China could have dreamed; she became the unofficial spokesperson for all of China soon after her first visit back to America since her 1917 graduation from Wellesley College in Massachusetts. While most of America was largely ignorant of anyone or anything Chinese, the ever elegant May-ling burst onto the scene speaking fluid English with just a hint of a Southern drawl imploring Americans to strengthen their relationship with China even more in order to fight against Japan. As her picture increasingly graced the pages of American newspapers and her eloquent speeches flowed into their living rooms via the new technology of radio, the third daughter of Charlie Soong would become one of the most recognizable faces in America, and one of the most crucial and influential figures in the history of Chinese-American relations (her photo appeared on the cover of *Time* magazine several times).

The influence of the Soong family on Chinese-American relations during and after World War II, however, would not be limited May-ling. Indeed, it has become a historical irony that while May-ling Soong became the poster child of harmonious Chinese-American relations during World War II, she never held much in the way of an official government position in China or America. That responsibility would instead go to her older brother, T. V. Soong.

Tse-Ven Soong, Charlie's oldest son, never quite attained the same level of long-lasting, universal popularity in America as his younger sister, May-ling, but he was just as well-known and even more influential in the field of international politics in the years before and after World War II. After graduating from Harvard with a degree in economics, T. V. worked briefly in banking in New York, then returned to China. He began his political career there by first working as a secretary for Sun Yat-sen (several years after his father's death), thereby continuing what was a Soong family tradition. Eventually his connection to Sun led to a position with Chiang Kai-shek's government as finance minister in the 1930s (Sun Yat-sen died in 1925) and governor of the Central Bank of China. During this time he also established the National Economic Council for the purpose of promoting industrialization in China and established the first stock market in Shanghai.

After a break of several years from Chiang Kai-shek and his Nationalist government in China, T. V. was again in the spotlight after being appointed minister of foreign affairs for Chiang's Nationalist government in China. Because of the position, he would spend most of his time during World War II living and working in Washington, D. C., to gain both financial and political support for China. Although Japan's defeat in 1945 led to much celebration in China, it was short-lived. Almost as soon as Japan surrendered in 1945, China descended into even deeper turmoil and conflict in the form of a civil war between Chiang Kai-shek (leading the Nationalists) and Mao Ze-Dong (leading the Communists). When Chiang was forced to flee to Taiwan in 1949, T. V. Soong fled to the United States, where he remained until his death in 1971.

Charlie's daughter Ching-ling, who was the wife of Sun Yat-sen, would never attain much fame in America, but in her native country her status would become legendary. Despite the fact that Sun Yat-sen would die in 1925 after only ten years of marriage to her, her unofficial status as "Mother of the Nation" would elevate her to near demi-god status in China for the remainder of her life. Her popularity, however, as well as her ever-increasing dislike of her brother-in-law Chiang Kai-shek, would create some tense family dynamics in the years to come. Sadly for the legacy of Charlie Soong and his wife, few families paid the price more publicly for their involvement in twentieth century Chinese politics than the Soongs. The family that was once a model of cross-cultural solidarity and of China's educational and economic potential would transform into a symbol of China's fractured identity and seeming perpetual conflict.

The 1930s and 40s were complicated, confusing, and difficult times in China, but Soong Ching-ling would remain a popular public figure throughout, especially in regards to her opposition to Chiang Kai-shek and his followers, and in regards to her many achievements at the time, including leading the China League for Civil Rights and the China Defense League. When Chiang was forced to retreat to Taiwan in 1949, Ching-ling was faced with a decision regarding China's first Communist government. While the communists were only all to eager to get their stamp of approval from Ching-ling and gain her loyalty, Ching-ling became increasingly supportive of them, leading many Chinese outside of China to label her a traitor. As the years passed, she would serve in various posts in the service of China's government, and was known to have occasionally expressed controversial statements toward the United States in political speeches. She would also adopt two daughters and remain an outspoken advocate of equal rights in China.

Ching-ling's death in 1981 brought about a tremendous outpouring of support for her in China, including the official designation of honorary president of the People's Republic of China during the final days of her life. The decision to bury her with her parents in Shanghai cemetery rather than with her husband,

Sun Yat-sen, in Nanjing was an unusual one (typically only single woman were buried with their parents in Chinese culture), but it was not entirely a surprising one.

Soong Ai-ling married H. H. Kung (孔祥熙), one of the most prestigious names one can have in China as it designates descendance from the noblest of noble individuals in all of Chinese history, Confucius. As a member of an extremely wealthy family, Kung's occupation as a banker and financier would make him one of the wealthiest men in China in the twentieth century. His ever-expanding role in the government administration of his brother-in-law, Chiang Kai-shek, throughout the 1930s and 40s, including stints as premiere of the Republic of China and minister of finance, assured him a spot in the public eye. Not surprisingly, H. H. and Ai-ling fled to the United States when Chiang Kai-shek and the Nationalists fled China to Taiwan in 1949. The two remaining Soong brothers never attained the public notoriety their elder siblings did, but perhaps they preferred it that way.

Charlie Soong perhaps wouldn't have been surprised that most of his descendants eventually moved to America. Though proud of his Chinese heritage, his years spent in America had a profound impact on both his identity and his outlook, and it was bound to influence his children. While he had much to be proud of, it is impossible to know whether or not he harbored any regrets in his latter years. According to some accounts, however, not even death and the passage of time could protect Charlie from the seemingly endless plague of violence and turmoil that plagued China in the twentieth century when his tomb was supposedly vandalized in the blind violence that visited China once again during the Cultural Revolution in the 1960s. Regardless of the questionable veracity of such accounts, Charlie's tomb was restored in later years following the death of his daughter, Ching-ling, who was subsequently buried alongside him and Mrs. Soong.

The fame he purposefully eschewed for so long did indeed turn out to be a double-edged sword for Charlie Soong, as did his relationship with Sun Yat-sen. There were some who worked as hard as Charlie in the name of revolution in China, but there were not nearly as many who willingly laid everything on the line, including their lives and the lives of their own family members, for the sake of China's future. Charlie worked so hard and risked so much with the confidence that China could lift itself out of the decades-long morass into which it had descended. He was elated beyond words and more optimistic than ever when the revolution finally succeeded and the Qing dynasty quietly faded into oblivion. As reality set in, however, and chaos soon again descended upon China in the years after the revolution, his hopes for a new and better China must have continually waxed and waned.

Charlie's falling out with Sun Yat-sen during the last decade of his life was unfortunate for both him and China. It is almost impossible to know how he personally felt about Sun in his final years, but it really doesn't matter. As Sun became a larger than life hero in the years after the 1911 Revolution, anybody who came into conflict with him or threatened the cult of personality that gradually built up around him in China in the decades after his death was quietly dropped from Chinese history books and erased from government records. Regardless of Sun Yat-sen's popularity, it can't be argued that Charlie Soong was not justified in his anger at Sun, or that Sun's conduct in his personal life did not have the potential to interfere with the success and legacy of the revolution in China. Indeed, influential

Christian communities around the world took great pride in the fact that Sun Yat-sen, and later, Chiang Kai-shek, were baptized Christians; any highly publicized behavior on their part that strongly conflicted with long-established Christian mores was bound to bring about broader scrutiny.

In the bigger picture, however, Charlie likely would not have minded his dearth of fame in twentieth century China. He may have achieved great success in his latter years, but he maintained an air of humility and gratitude throughout his life, and likely enjoyed his years out of the spotlight more than the unwelcome fame he acquired later in life anyway. The fact that his name and reputation are slowly being restored in China among historians and intellectuals is perhaps all the gratitude that Charlie Soong would have ever asked for.

BIBLIOGRAPHY

Bergere, Marie-Claire. *Sun Yat Sen.* Stanford: Stanford University Press, 1998.

Burke, James. *My Father In China.* New York: Farrar & Rinehart, Inc., 1942.

Cantlie, James. *Sun Yat-sen and the Awakening of China.* Jarrold & Sons; 1920.

Chang, Iris. *The Chinese In America.* New York: Viking Press, 2003.

Chesneaux, Jean (editor). *Popular Movements and Secret Societies in China 1840-1950.* Stanford: Stanford University Press, 1972.

Clark, Elmer T. *The Chiangs of China.* New York: Abingdon-Cokesbury Press, 1943.

Cohen, Lucy M. *Chinese In the Post-Civil War South.* Baton Rouge: Louisiana State University Press, 1984.

Cohen, Paul A. *Between Tradition and Modernity: Wang Tao and Reform in Late Ch'ing China.* Cambridge: Harvard University Press, 1974.

Compilation Committee. *A Pictorial History of the Republic of China—Its Founding and Development (Two Volumes).* Taipei: Modern China Press, 1981.

David M. Rubenstein Rare Book and Manuscript Library, Duke University. *Charles Jones Soong Reference Collection.*

Delong, Thomas A. *Madame Chiang Kai-shek and Miss Emma Mills: China's First Lady and Her American Friend.* Jefferson, NC: McFarland, 2007.

Dowd, Jerome. *Life of Braxton Craven.* Raleigh: Edwards & Broughton, 1896.

Dowd, Jerome. *Life of Braxton Craven: A Biological Approach to Social Science.* Durham, Duke University Press, 1939.

Green, C. Sylvester (editor). *General Julian S. Carr, Greathearted Citizen.* Durham: Seeman Printery, 1945.

Hahn, Emily. *The Soong Sisters.* New York: Doubleday, Doran, & Co., 1941.

Leibovitz, Liel, and Matthew Miller, *Fortunate Sons.* New York: W.W. Norton & Co., 2011.

Lo Hui-Min (editor). *The Correspondence of G.E. Morrison II, 1912-1920.* New York: Cambridge University Press, 1976.

Pakula, Hannah. *The Last Empress: Madame Chiang Kai-shek and the Birth of Modern China.* New York: Simon & Schuster, 2009.

Restarick, Henry Bond. *Sun Yat Sen, Liberator of China.* New Haven: Yale University Press, 1931.

Schriffrin, Harold Z. *Sun Yat-Sen, Reluctant Revolutionary*. Boston: Little, Brown, and Co., 1980.

Seagrave, Sterling. *The Soong Dynasty*. New York: Corgi Books, 1996.

Selle, Earl Albert. *Donald of China*. New York: Harper, 1948.

Snow, Edgar. *Journey to the Beginning*. New York: Random House, 1958.

Spence, Jonathan. *The Search for Modern China*. New York: Norton, 1990.

Spence, Jonathan. *The Memory Palace of Matteo Ricci*. New York: Viking Penguin, 1984.

Tsang, Steve. *A Modern History of Hong Kong*. London: I. B. Tauris, 2007.

Webb, Mena. *Jule Carr*. Chapel Hill: University of North Carolina Press, 1987.

Wilbur, Clarence Martin. *Sun Yat-Sen, Frustrated Patriot*. New York: Columbia University Press, 1976.

Wing, Yung. *My Life in China and America*. London: Forgotten Books, 2012.

Young, Ernest P. *The Presidency of Yuan Shi-k'ai*. Ann Arbor: University of Michigan Press, 1977.

NOTES

CHAPTER ONE: Boston Calling

1. Information regarding Charlie, his relationship with Captain Gabrielson, and his experience aboard the *Albert Gallatin* are extracted from the 1943 Coast Guard Report, *"Charles Jones Soong and Captain Eric Gabrielson: A Footnote to World History."* Courtesy *Charles Jones Soong Reference Collection*, David M. Rubenstein Rare Book and Manuscript Library, Duke University.

2. Details regarding Charlie's birth name and his birthplace are found in the *Xin Hua News Agency* newspaper article on October 17, 2010, "秘史：宋慶齡宋美齡其實不姓宋" ("Secret History: Soong Qing Ling and Soong Mei-ling Are Not Actually Named "Soong").

3. Charlie's age has been the subject of much past debate. The date of October 17, 1861 is now generally accepted by scholars in China as Charlie's birthday. See the October 17, 2011 *China News Service* article, "宋氏家族奠基人耀如：曾愤怒庆领嫁孙中山" ("Soong Family Founder Soong Yao Ru: Anger at Qing-ling's Marriage to Sun Yat-sen").

4. Details about Charlie's "adoption" and subsequent name change are from the October 17, 2011 *China News Service* article.

5. Charlie's 1878 arrival in Boston is from a letter written to his parents. The letter is from James Burke, *My Father in China* (1942), p. 8.

6. Charlie's life in Boston and his relationship with B.C. Wen and N.C. New are chronicled in Emily Hahn, *The Soong Sisters* (1941), p. 5. A dose of skepticism regarding popular accounts of Charlie's early life in America is often appropriate as they are sometimes difficult to verify. The influence of Wen and

New on Charlie is one such account. Their supposed friendship in Boston has become part of popular lore owing largely to the publication of Hahn's book in 1941, but it was published over twenty years after Charlie's death.

7. Neither Wen nor New ever actually lived in Boston, but in outlying cities like Amherst and Springfield roughly one hundred miles away. It is entirely possible, however, that occasional train trips into Boston were made by both Wen and New. Regardless, their friendship later in life is well documented. An ambitious website dedicated to the Chinese Educational Mission can be found at http://www.cemconnections.org.

8. Details about Charlie's service in the U. S. Revenue Marine are from a Coast Guard report commissioned in 1943, the purpose of which was to find out the details of Charlie Soong's background. Charlie's son, T. V., was serving as a sort of de facto Chinese ambassador to the United States at the time. Courtesy *Charles Jones Soong Reference Collection,* David M. Rubenstein Rare Book and Manuscript Library, Duke University.

9. Facts pertaining to China's population and other nineteenth century problems are from Jonathan Spence, *The Search for Modern China* (1991), p. 94.

10. The list of problems facing China and resultant rebellions are discussed in Spence, p. 139.

CHAPTER TWO: A Wilmington Welcome

1. The intriguing accounts of some of the first Chinese in America are in Iris Chang, *The Chinese in America* (2004), p. 26.

2. Yung Wing information is from Spence, p. 198.

3. Information about the Foreign Miner's Tax can be found at the Online Archive of California at http://www.oac.cdlib.org.

4. The aforementioned 1943 Coast Guard Report contains details about Captain Gabrielson's transfer to Wilmington, N.C., as well as Charlie's request for dismissal from service and his subsequent move to Wilmington.

5. Information about the Chang and Eng Bunker is found in Chang, p. 27-28.

6. "Crazy Kitty" is from the Wilmington *Morning Star,* July 23, 1880. Courtesy of the Archives at New Hanover County Public Library.

7. "Well-behaved Wilmington" is from the Wilmington *Morning Star,* January 14, 1881. Courtesy of the Archives at New Hanover County Public Library.

8. "Twenty Five Cent Robbery" is from the Wilmington *Morning Star,* August 28, 1880. Courtesy of the Archives at New Hanover County Public Library.

9. Part of the challenge in verifying who was responsible for originally befriending Charlie and pointing him in the direction of the Fifth Avenue Methodist Church lies in the fact that Charlie perhaps would have been long forgotten in Wilmington if his children (esp. Madame Chiang Kai-shek; a.k.a Soong Mei-ling) had not become celebrities in the 1930s and 40s. The motivation to claim some connection to Charlie Soong at this time would have been strong for those who placed a high value on social status in the same way that a person today may boast of a friendship (real or imagined) with a celebrity or millionaire.

10. Lending credence to the Moore connection is the fact that he supposedly served in the Civil War in the same Confederate regiment as Julian Carr, the man who would later become

Charlie's generous benefactor (a relationship perhaps built on an introduction arranged by Moore). There is no doubt that Moore was at least a minor celebrity in Wilmington as on Sept. 25, 1885, the Wilmington *Morning Star* contains an article celebrating the naming of a local ship after Moore. The article describes Moore as a "well-known and popular citizen of Wilmington."

11. Information about Moore and Ricaud is from Elmer Clark, *The Chiangs of China* (1943), p. 14.

12. Mrs. Chadwick's and Mrs. Howell's account of Charlie's conversion is from "The Romance of Charlie Soong" in the *Duke Divinity School Bulletin,* vol. IV, no. 4 (Jan. 1942). Courtesy *Charles Jones Soong Reference Collection,* David M. Rubenstein Rare Book and Manuscript Library, Duke University.

13. The letter regarding the Southport account of Charlie's Christian conversion can be found in the *North Carolina Christian Advocate*, December 19, 1995. Courtesy *Charles Jones Soong Reference Collection,* David M. Rubenstein Rare Book and Manuscript Library, Duke University.

14. The November 9, 1880 account of Charlie's baptism is from the Wilmington *Morning Star.* Courtesy of the Archives at New Hanover County Public Library.

CHAPTER THREE: Student Meets Mentor

1. Information about old Durham is from Mena Webb, *Jule Carr* (1987), p. 30-34.

2. The University of North Carolina is often accepted as the oldest public university in the United States, but the University of Georgia and the College of William and Mary also lay claim to this title.

3. Durham and Chapel Hill during the days after the Appomattox surrender is from Webb, p. 21.
4. Info on Carr and his tobacco business success is from Webb, p. 67.
5. The article is from the Wilmington *Morning Star*, April 20, 1881. This article was discovered by the author during research and is believed to be unknown to historians (and the first time ever reprinted).
6. "…came forward for prayer, but…" is from James Southgate's "The History of Trinity United Church" found on the Trinity United Methodist Church website at http://www.trinitydurham.org.
7. Info about Charlie's intro to Carr is from a speech by Costen J. Harrell, and included in C. Sylvester Greene, *Greathearted Citizen* (1945), p. 61.
8. "Not as a servant….." is from Greene, p. 66.
9. Information about Trinity College and Trinity, North Carolina is from the city of Trinity website at http://www.trinity-nc.gov.
10. The difficulties faced by Trinity College in the late 1870s and early 1880s can be found in The *Charlotte Observer* article, "What Is Now Duke University Moved to Durham in Freight Car in 1892," published on March 19, 1950.
11. The letters Charlie wrote back to Dr. Allen and his father in Hainan are from Burke, p. 7. Burke's book, while extremely informative, is not an ideal reference resource as it contains no endnotes that provide information in regards to how he came into possession of these letters more than sixty years after they were written by Charlie. Burke does not say how he obtained these letters or from whom. That being said, Burke's occupation as a journalist/photographer for *Time Life* Magazine lends one to believe that

credibility was a priority in his writing. The letters do seem authentic and there is nothing about them that suggests they were fabrications.

12. "As early as 1854..." is from Lucy M. Cohen, *Chinese in the Post Civil War South* (1984), p. 22.
13. The 1869 labor convention in Memphis, Tennessee is mentioned in Cohen, p. 67.
14. Circumstances of Chinese laborers in Peru and Cuba is from Cohen, p. 28

CHAPTER FOUR: A Great Deal of Attention

1. "...never had but one ambition," is from Jerome Dowd, *Life of Braxton Craven, D.D. LL. D.* (1896), p. 94.
2. "...above all things," is from Dowd, p. 92
3. "He was a man..." is from Dowd, p. 78.
4. "Sometimes hearing of some mischief," is from Dowd, p. 81.
5. "His control over his students, " is from Dowd, p. 93.
6. Although Braxton Craven Middle School now sits on the original site of Trinity College, not a lot has changed in Trinity since the days of Charlie Soong's enrollment there. A small pavilion housing the original school bell of Trinity College peacefully sits peacefully in quiet repose along Route 62 in front of the middle school, interrupted only by the occasional passing of a car. Indeed, even Braxton Craven himself (along side his wife) still resides in the town's main cemetery just up the road from his former school.
7. The Halloween pumpkin story is from Hahn, p. 11.
8. "His stature was short..." is from Jerome Dowd, *The Life of Braxton Craven: A Biological Approach to Social Science* (1939), p. 196.
9. "...did not make much headway," *ibid*, p. 196

10. The letter written by Charlie in the spring of 1882 appears courtesy *Charles Jones Soong Reference Collection,* David M. Rubenstein Rare Book and Manuscript Library, Duke University.

11. Charlie's June 20, 1882 letter to J.G. Hackett appears courtesy *Charles Jones Soong Reference Collection,* David M. Rubenstein Rare Book and Manuscript Library, Duke University.

12. Ella Carr's photo and article about Charlie is from the September 1, 1937 edition of the Greensboro *Daily News* in an article entitled "High Point Resident Has Cherished Photo."

13. The minutes from the Sixteenth Session of the Hillsboro District Conference of the Methodist Episcopal Church that met on July 20, 1882 appear courtesy of *Charles Jones Soong Reference Collection,* David M. Rubenstein Rare Book and Manuscript Library, Duke University.

14. The theory that Charlie was suddenly transferred to Vanderbilt because of a tryst with Ella Carr seems largely the product of popular imagination. It seems to be based solely on the 1937 interview with Ella Carr in which she mentions that Charlie used to come to her house often to hear her play piano, but that her mother told him to stop coming around so much, and the fact that Charlie mailed her a photo of himself from Nashville.

15. All quotes pertaining to Braxton Craven's health are from Jerome Dowd, p. 106-7. Piedmont Springs information can be found in the Duke University Library Digital Collection at http://library.duke.edu/digitalcollections/broadsides_bdsnc031712/.

16. Quotes about Charlie's departure from the Cravens are from an article in the *Raleigh News & Observer* by Mike Bradshaw, "Chinese Lad Left Trinity College to Found Own Dynasty," June 28, 1936.

17. Details about the Self-Strengthening movement are from Spence, *The Search for Modern China* (1990), p. 197.

18. Details about young Sun Yat-sen and his brother in Hawaii are extracted from Marie-Claire Bergere, *Sun Yat-sen*, p. 24.

19. "….attendance at daily prayers" is from Bergere, p. 25.

CHAPTER FIVE: So Alone Among Strangers

1. Details about the early days of Vanderbilt University are from the Vanderbilt University website at http://www.vanderbilt.edu/about/history.

2. Mention of the 1890s fire at Vanderbilt is in a letter to Mrs. A. Sharman from Vanderbilt Alumni Secretary Hill Turner dated September 22, 1931. Courtesy Vanderbilt University Archives.

3. "He was of a most genial…" is from Hahn, p. 9.

4. "…of a jovial disposition," *ibid*, p. 9.

5. "…prepared his lessons well," is from "The Romance of Charlie Soong," p. 76.

6. 'Some of the Wesley boys…" is from "The Romance of Charlie Soong," p. 76-77.

7. "He was not a highly successful…" is from Edwin Mims, *History of Vanderbilt University* (1946), p. 175.

8. The story of the electric flat iron prank at Vanderbilt is from Burke, p. 4-5.

9. "…wild living and overindulgence" is from Spence, *The Search for Modern China* (1990), p. 216.

10. "Everything in the village…" is from Bergere, p. 25

11. Sun Yat-sen's enrollment at the Hong Kong Government Central School is from Bergere, p. 26.

CHAPTER SIX: The Easy Chair

1. Charlie's letter to Dr. Allen is from Burke, p. 10.
2. The letter Charlie wrote from Vanderbilt to Annie Southgate in Durham appears courtesy *Charles Jones Soong Reference Collection,* David M. Rubenstein Rare Book and Manuscript Library, Duke University.
3. Charlie's letter to the *Raleigh Christian Advocate* on May 13, 1885 appears courtesy *Charles Jones Soong Reference Collection,* David M. Rubenstein Rare Book and Manuscript Library, Duke University.
4. Reverend McTyiere's letter to Reverend Allen in Shanghai is from Burke, p. 12.
5. George Winton's comments are from Bradshaw.
6. Details regarding Charlie's "English Theological Certificate" are from the 1931 letter to Mrs. A. Sharman from Vanderbilt Alumni Secretary Hill Turner.
7. "I have been preaching some…" is from "The Romance of Charlie Soong," p. 77.
8. "Some years ago…" is courtesy of New Hanover county Public Library archives.
9. "Alluding to Charlie Soong…" is courtesy of New Hanover County Public Library Archives.
10. Reverend Ricaud's service record at the First United Methodist Church of Washington can be found on that church's website at http://www.fumcw.com/?page_id=382. He was minister at FUMCW from 1883-1886.
11. Charlie's letter to Annie Southgate, dated July 18, 1885, was written in Plymouth, North Carolina. It appears courtesy *Charles Jones Soong Reference Collection,* David M. Rubenstein Rare Book and Manuscript Library, Duke University.

12. Miss Bell (Mrs. Rowe's) recollections of Charlie are from "When Charlie Soong Paid a Visit to Washington, *NC*" by Pauline Worthy from the *Raleigh News & Observer*, Feb 28, 1943.
13. Charlie's visit to Reverend Tuttle in Wilmington in 1885 is from Bradshaw.
14. Details about the anti-Chinese riots in Tacoma, Washington can be found online at http://www.historylink.org/index.cfm?DisplayPage=output.cfm&file_id=5063.
15. The plea for missionaries articles is from the *Raleigh Christian Advocate*, October 21, 1885.
16. The minutes of the 1885 North Carolina Annual Conference of the M.E. Church are in the *Raleigh Christian Advocate*, December 2, 1885. Under the heading "Third Day" Charlie's name is listed among others as being admitted to the ministry on a "trial" basis. Courtesy *Charles Jones Soong Reference Collection,* David M. Rubenstein Rare Book and Manuscript Library, Duke University.
17. Details about the impact of the Sino-French War on Hong Kong are from Steve Tsang, *A Modern History of Hong Kong* (2007), p. 91.
18. Names and amounts of money given to Sun Yat-sen are from the website http://www.sunyatsenhawaii.org.
19. "Sun had probably encouraged him…" is from Bergere, p. 27.

CHAPTER SEVEN: A Foreigner in China
1. The letter to the *Raleigh Christian Advocate* was written by Charlie in Soochow, China on February 27, 1886. It did not appear in the *Raleigh Christian Advocate* until April 14, 1886. It is believed by the author that its appearance in this book is the first time

the letter has ever been reprinted anywhere. Courtesy *Charles Jones Soong Reference Collection,* David M. Rubenstein Rare Book and Manuscript Library, Duke University.

2. The story of C.K. Marshall is from Burke, p. 33.

3. An alternative version of this story has Mr. Lambuth, Charlie's well respected missionary friend, befriending C.K. Marshall when he was a boy in Shanghai just after his father died. According to this account, it was Lambuth who took Marshall to America with him and later introduced him to Dr. D.C. Kelley, also a missionary with much experience in China.

4. Yung Wing's account of returning to China after several years in America and realizing that he forgot how to speak Chinese is in his memoir, *My Life in China and America,* p. 48.

5. Much information about Matteo Ricci can be gleaned from Jonathan Spence, *The Memory Palace of Matteo Ricci* (1983).

6. Details about Dr. Allen and his achievements in China are from Burke, p. 35.

7. Dr. Allen's letter to the Mission Board is from Burke, p. 34.

8. Charlie's letter to the *Raleigh Christian Advocate,* printed on July 7, 1886, appears courtesy *Charles Jones Soong Reference Collection,* David M. Rubenstein Rare Book and Manuscript Library, Duke University.

9. Charlie's letter to "My dearest Friend" back in Durham was dated June 14, 1886 and was sent from Suzhou, China. Courtesy *Charles Jones Soong Reference Collection,* David M. Rubenstein Rare Book and Manuscript Library, Duke University.

10. Charlie's letter to the *Raleigh Christian Advocate* was printed on August 4, 1886. Courtesy *Charles Jones Soong Reference Collection,* David M. Rubenstein Rare Book and Manuscript Library, Duke University.

CHAPTER EIGHT: Friends Old and New

1. "…drawn up by Chinese philanthropists…" is from Pakula, p. 35.
2. Details about the "light ladies" of Shanghai and the Japanese ships that transported them there can be found in Burke, p. 210.
3. "There was never much left…" is from Burke, p. 212.
4. Dr. Hu Shi's comments about Charlie are from Bradshaw.
5. Charlie's October 7, 1886 letter to Mr. Southgate appears courtesy of *Charles Jones Soong Reference Collection,* David M. Rubenstein Rare Book and Manuscript Library, Duke University.
6. Charlie's February 4, 1887 letter to Mr. Southgate appears courtesy *Charles Jones Soong Reference Collection,* David M. Rubenstein Rare Book and Manuscript Library, Duke University.
7. "Well, sakes alive, Charlie!..." is from Burke, p. 30.
8. Charlie's failed courtship efforts and Miss Lockie Rankin's involvement are from Burke, p. 33.
9. Charlie's December 21, 1887 letter (announcing his marriage) to the *Raleigh Christian Advocate* appears courtesy of *Charles Jones Soong Reference Collection,* David M. Rubenstein Rare Book and Manuscript Library, Duke University.
10. Details about Ms Ni's family history are from Burke, p. 37.
11. "*The Tobacco Plant…*" appears courtesy of New Hanover County Public Library Archives.
12. Details regarding Sun Yat-Sen and his student years in Hong Kong are from Bergere, p. 31.

CHAPTER NINE: Breaking Away

1. "Two foreign devils…" is from Burke, p. 51.
2. Details about Burke's visit with Charlie in Kunshan are from Burke, p. 51.

3. "Sometimes I think I could do...." is from Burke, p. 54.

4. Information about the American Bible Society is from its website at http://www.americanbible.org.

5. Evidence that Charlie ever worked in a Wilmington, NC print shop is extremely scant. Mention of it is found only in a single article, "General Carr and The Education of Charlie Soong," written six decades after Charlie lived in North Carolina and originally published in *The World Outlook*, but later reprinted in the Raleigh *News and Observer* on October 14, 1945. Costen J. Harrell, the author, was a North Carolina Methodist bishop who also claims to have briefly served as secretary to Julian Carr while a young man. As far as the assertion that Julian Carr personally financed Charlie's printing business is concerned, it is possible, but there exists no evidence to support this supposition other than Harrell's statement.

6. Details about Wang Tao's life are in Paul A. Cohen, *Between Tradition and Modernity: Wang T'ao and Reform in Late Ch'ing China* (1975).

7. Charlie's angry letter to the *Raleigh Christian Advocate* was printed on October 19, 1892 and appears courtesy *Charles Jones Soong Reference Collection,* David M. Rubenstein Rare Book and Manuscript Library, Duke University.

8. Details about Sun Yat-sen's career prospects are from Bergere, p. 37.

9. " I have passed English..." is from Bergere, p. 40.

10. An excellent source of information about the history of secret societies in China can be found in Jean Chesneaux's *Popular Movements and Secret Societies in China, 1840-1950.*

11. Details surrounding the founding of Sun Yat-sen's Xing Zhong Hui are from Berege, p. 50.

CHAPTER TEN: A Revolutionary Is Born

1. "He was very frank and outspoken…" is from Hahn, as are all subsequent quotes pertaining to the view of Charlie as unorthodox in Shanghai, pp. 27-29.
2. Charlie's donation of three thousand yuan is from the October 17, 2011 *China News Service* article.
3. "…whenever he came to Shanghai," is from Hahn, p. 25.
4. Cantlie's account of his run in with Sun Yat-sen in Hawaii is from James Cantlie, *Sun Yat-sen and the Awakening of China*, p. 39.
5. "There is a friend of yours imprisoned…" is from Cantlie, p. 42.
6. Details about Ai-ling's trip to America with Burke are from Burke, p. 229.
7. The article concerning Ai-ling's visit to Durham is from the *Durham Daily Sun*, July 20, 1904.
8. B.C. Wen's career is chronicled at the CEM website at http://cemconnections.org
9. "America is very beautiful…" is from Hahn, p. 49.
10. "…IOU's for very high interest loans" is from Bergere, p. 191.
11. "…from October 1905 to February 1906" is from Bergere, p. 191.
12. The figure of two million dollars raised by Charlie is from the October 17, 2011 *China News Service* article.
13. Details about Charlie's 1905 visit to Durham are from Bradshaw.

CHAPTER ELEVEN: An Unexpected Triumph

1. "Cool and inviting…retreat," is from Earl Albert Selle, Donald of China (1948), p. 67
2. Well! How is Australia's…" is from Selle, p. 68.
3. The American missionary's account of Charlie's reaction to the Wuchang Uprising and the beginning of the Chinese

Revolution is from a 1942 Upton Close radio show transcript in which the unnamed missionary describes her friendship with Charlie in Shanghai several decades earlier. There is some evidence that the last name of the missionary was Roberts. Courtesy *Charles Jones Soong Reference Collection,* David M. Rubenstein Rare Book and Manuscript Library, Duke University.

4. Sun's explanation of his whereabouts in the days after the Wuchang Uprising is from Selle, p. 110.
5. Sun Yat-sen's delay in returning to China after the Wuchang Uprising is from Bergere, p, 207.
6. "American generals…" is from Selle, p. 107.
7. "Chinese people do not like…" is from Selle, p. 109.
8. Sun Yat-sen's letter (April 17, 1912) to Mr. Li about Charlie Soong is from the October 17, 2011 edition of *The China News* in the article "The Soong Family Founder Soong Yaoru: Anger at Qing-ling's Marriage to Sun Yat-sen" by Zhou Wei Min. The article was written partly in celebration of the one hundredth anniversary of the 1911 Revolution and partly in celebration of the one-hundred fiftieth anniversary of Charlie Soong's birth. Information in the article was derived from a conference of scholars that was convened on the island of Hainan, Charlie's birthplace, as part of the celebration.

CHAPTER TWELVE: First Cracks
1. Details pertaining to Sun Yat-sen's marriage proposal to Ai-ling are from Selle, p. 139-140.
2. The Tokyo train station encounter with Charlie Soong is from the 1942 Upton Close transcript. Courtesy *Charles Jones*

Soong Reference Collection, David M. Rubenstein Rare Book and Manuscript Library, Duke University.

3. Charlie's first letter (May 3, 1915) from Japan to his son, T.V., in America appears courtesy of *Charles Jones Soong Reference Collection,* David M. Rubenstein Rare Book and Manuscript Library, Duke University.

4. Charlie's second letter (August 6, 1915) from Japan to his son in America appears courtesy *Charles Jones Soong Reference Collection,* David M. Rubenstein Rare Book and Manuscript Library, Duke University.

CHAPTER THIRTEEN: Surprise Endings

1. R.R. Gailey letter to G.E. Morrison is from Lo Hui Min (ed.), *The Correspondence of G. E. Morrison 1912-1920,* p. 477.

2. Enclosure to letter No. 792 is from Lo, p. 478

3. 148 Julian Carr's letter from Manila is from the article "General Carr Writes Letter" in the *Morning Herald* on March 22, 1917 (Durham, North Carolina).

4. Excerpts from Julian Carr's diary are courtesy of the University of North Carolina Archives.

5. "Bill, I was never so hurt…" is from Burke, p. 265.

6. "Mother says she does not…" is from *Madame Chiang Kai-shek and Miss Emma Mills,* p.19.

7. Charlie's July 5, 1918 *Wilmington Dispatch* obituary appears courtesy of New Hanover County Public Library Archives.

INDEX

—◦◦◦—

Ho Kai, p. 87
Hongkew, p. 139
Hong Kong (anti-French riots), p. 84
Hong Kong College of Medicine for the Chinese, p. 118, 130
Hong Kong University, p. 85
Hong Xiu Quan, p. 13
Hundred Days of Reform, p. 158-159
Hu Shi, Dr., p. 105

immigrants, Chinese, p. 15-17
Iolani School, p. 57

Jones (in reference to Charlie Soong's middle name), p. 25, 30-31

Kelley, Dr. D.C., p. 93
Kung, H.H., p. 183, 186, 189, 190, 204
Kunshan, China, p. 105, 114, 121
Kuomintang (KMT) Party, p. 175

labor convention (for recruiting Chinese workers to the American
    South), p. 40
Lea, Homer, p. 165-167
Lee, Daniel, p. 39
Ligure (ship), p. 3
Li Xiao Sheng, p. 169
London Missionary Society, p. 85
Lu Haodong, p. 65, 140, 169

Macon, GA, p. 149
Madame Chiang Kai-shek, see Soong May-ling
Manchu, p. 118-119, 140, 161, 167, 170-171